The Planets Align So Rare:
Twelve Dimensions to the Human Potential

Ray Sette
with Carlo DeCarlo

Outskirts Press, Inc.
Denver, Colorado

The Planets Align So Rare:
Twelve Dimensions to the Human Potential
All Rights Reserved

Outskirts Press
http://www.outskirtspress.com
ISBN-10: 1-59800-720-3
ISBN-13: 978-1-59800-720-6

This book is dedicated to my parents,
Giovanna & Giuseppe Sette

For bringing me into this World
so that I might have this opportunity
of choosing to realize
my human potential.

I love you very much~

...Raymond

Special Thanks...

To Carlo:
For taking my words and crafting them
so this world can hear my voice.
My *Brother of the Moon*, my oldest and dearest friend,
you have stayed with me through my darkest hours...
You have never forsaken me~
I love you dearly...

To Giancarlo:
For helping me realize my strength
and physical potential
~and a lifetime of treasured memories.

To Susanne & Karen:
My Sisters of the Moon.

To James:
My "other" brother.

To Billy:
For the Sea, the Sunsets and the Shooting Stars.

To Aileen:
"Is Love so fragile, and the heart so hollow..."

To Dr. Bob & Evelyn:
For keeping me "straight" all these years.

To Pam:
For my sanctuary by the Sea.

To Olivia:
For seeing something in my smile…
and trusting a stranger~

To Stephanie:
As you once sang;
"I cannot live without your songs…"

To Jodelle:
Only you and I know what we have overcome and
endured so that we may realize our Dreams…
and for being one of the first with whom
I chose to share these words.

To Ginger, Linda & Connie:
My "Three of Cups"

To Therese:
For taking the time to read my work,
and of course…*the Sea.*

To Annmarie:
For your tireless efforts in reviewing this material.

And, of course…

Andreas~
My littlest Wizard~

*…and to the Dreamers
Who choose to Believe~
So that this World
will be a better place…
In Love & Light,
~Ray*

Contents

Introduction

*The world is round and the place
which may seem like the end
may also be only the beginning.*
—IVY BARKER PRIEST

IN THE BEGINNING...

L ife never really begins; it just always has been. The beginning of our existence and experience in human form may perhaps commence at the moment of conception, or the moment we emerge from the womb, or the moment we take our first breath, or all of the above. However, the essence of that which we are has always been in continuum. All our human potential already lies within the fabric of our being; we need only to choose to make it real. For many years, I have been firm in the belief that at any moment of any day, we are at choice as to how we create our realities. More and more, we, as a people, are being clued in to this little secret. But how did it all begin–or has it always just *been*?

Our solar system was created from a massive ball of spiraling gas. Spinning, spinning, spinning. Imploding and exploding. Breathing in and breathing out. In each and every one of us, there is a piece of that original form. We are the particles of that whole, just like the massive ball of hydrogen gas that fuels the flames of the Sun, and the light that travels from the Sun to fuel the Earth–warming, nourishing, illuminating–yet remains a part of that whole carrying within it the essence of the Sun.

I am not an astrophysicist, so bear with me as I explain my understanding of the creation of our solar system (with an emphasis on "my understanding").

It is beyond our comprehension to fathom the infinite and eternal existence of the Universe, so as much as we are an integral part of it, how, in all our simplicity, can we grasp something so all-encompassing? Our planetary group is but one miniscule part of the great "All That Is." This solar system primarily consists of the nine known planets, the Sun, and our close satellite, the Moon. As I have suggested and will attempt to explicate, there is something within each of us that exists in every part of every planet and in every stray molecule in the Universe. Simply put, we are particles of that great whole, the Allness, the All That Is.

Our solar system began to form from a monstrous cloud of gas and dust, which contracted into a smaller–completely relative to the enormity of the Universe–cloud of dust and gas that eventually concentrated itself in the center. Ferociously spinning, once this center became stabilized, it gave birth to smaller clumps of gas, all of which were a part of that great whole. Those smaller clumps, spiraling around the larger, began to contract and compress. As these spawns moved away from the larger clump, which became a magnificent display of nuclear fission, they began to spin on their own, cool, and become dense. Their own uniqueness was taking shape.

They became individuals, and yet their essence remained connected to that original composition. They were not separate from one another; the life vibration of each of the individuals pulsated within each of them allowing them to share a bond that would never be broken.

As the individuations of the greater whole spun independently, they, too, produced their own offspring, which we would call moons. And those moons, in and of themselves, retained the properties of their original source and remained connected through a cosmic bond, which is part of the greater bond, which is part of the whole. Can you see the perfection and symmetry of this great orchestration of divinity?

So was the birth of our solar system.

WHAT IF GOD WERE ONE OF US?

God, Allah, Mecca, Buddha, Kyrie. They are really all the same. In the mid '90's, singer Joan Osbourne posed the question: "What if God was one of us, just a slob like one of us, just a stranger on the bus, trying to make his way home?" I would say, yes, God *is* one of us! She is a slob like one of us, and he is that stranger on the bus. I'm not one to quote the Bible, but in this instance I think I will allow myself. Was it not stated in the Bible that we are "made in the image and likeness of God?" So, God really could be one of us if that passage were to hold true. That homeless man on the street, the teacher who educates our children, the chiropractor who keeps our physical bodies aligned with the Universe, and the terrorist who hijacks a plane. Although, in hijacking a plane, for whatever reason, is that terrorist truly demonstrating the highest expression of human potential or simply the horror that may exist in each of us?

If we are to follow the Bible, these embodiments are all made in the image and likeness of God. This may also suggest that we have the creative power that was used to create the heavens and the Earth. So, why can't we reach our potential and create the true realities we desire?

It really doesn't matter who we worship or which religion's deity we consider to be "God." Isn't it of greater significance for a person to hold himself accountable for his own actions and accept the consequences of said actions, and how those actions influence the wholeness of humanity? To put it more plainly, what goes around, comes around. Whether it is obvious to us or not, our actions really do affect one another. From something as simple as a negative thought, spoken or unspoken, to something as grand as war, we are touched on some level. I use this simple metaphor: if one casts a stone into a pond, the ripples move outward to the greater parts of that pond–all parts have been touched, affected. The same holds true of our thoughts and actions.

I will not debate who or what God really is, for there is an abundance of material available for those who seek the possibilities to those questions and I feel we in our humanness with a sometimes blurred vision cannot see and comprehend "all that is encompassing." I can only express my personal designs of what or whom I would consider the entity known as God to exist as a result of my life's experiences. I also feel that in our limited vocabulary, there cannot be a true and accurate expression to define the essence of that which we call God, for that definition is very personal and specific to the individual, and thus no one specific ideology could be called "right" or "wrong."

I have come to know that God is in each and every person, plant, and animal. He is in every creature that lives and breathes the life force here on Earth (and in those far off places in the Universe) because she is that which created the life force. God is in Nature, and Nature is God. God is.

WHY TWELVE DIMENSIONS?

Why did I choose twelve dimensions? To be precise, I did not choose the number but rather I was instructed that twelve would be the perfect number for this material. Twelve relates to the twelve signs of the Zodiac and the twelve houses of the Astrological wheel. Twelve correlates with spirituality, the essence as it pertains to the world that is not of the physical but that of the spirit. The complete outline of this book was created in twelve weeks and the creation of the body of the book completed in another twelve. Twelve is the number of Governmental perfection. There were twelve tribes of Israel, twelve Apostles, twelve foundations in the heavenly Jerusalem, twelve gates, twelve pearls, twelve angels. The measurements of New Jerusalem are 12,000 furlongs, while the wall will be 144 [12 x 12] cubits (Rev. 21:16-17).

As you can see, twelve is universal; twelve allows for the perfect complement and balance of all things.

SYNCHRONICITY

In *Synchronicity: An Acausal Connecting Principle*, Carl Jung wrote, on his theory of synchronicity, that "...a thing or person born at a particular moment in time takes on the characteristics of that moment in time." It's no coincidence, then, that he was a longtime student and investigator of astrology, for, like in his theory of synchronicity, at the moment we enter this world–the precise date, time and location on the

Earth–the planets in our solar system form an astrological configuration that is as individual as a snowflake. That particular planetary arrangement may not be duplicated for millennia, hence, our individuality. Of course, we are always at choice as to how that individuality will be created and expressed, for at any moment, we demonstrate free will. Just as the Moon influences the ebb and flow of the tides, so the planets have their influence upon our beings. At any moment, we are at choice in how we are creating our realities in co-creation with the universe along with the gentle tugging of the heavenly bodies of our solar system.

If we were to look to the east at the moment when we took our first breath, we would have seen rising up from the east point of the horizon one of the twelve constellations. Astrologically, we refer to this as our rising sign or the Ascendant. The other eleven constellations of the zodiac then follow in succession. Many of us know our Sun sign, which is the sign of the zodiac the Sun resides in at the time we are born. However, that is only one small part of our astrological composition, for all the twelve signs and all the nine planets and the Moon, as well as some lesser heavenly bodies such as asteroids, have their own individual and specific place in our cosmic being.

Some of the planets may have been positioned above the horizon when we were born, some below. Some are not visible and some shine as brilliantly as a diamond in the sky. We may not always see these celestial spheres;

however, their aura and influence are omnipresent.

So, at that great moment of our physical birth, the die was cast: our astrological pattern, the indelible imprint on our Earthly form. We begin the process by choosing the specific time and place unto which we are born so that we can experience ourselves as both creator and co-creator with the All That Is. This power is within all of us, if we so choose to see it. And in these pages, I will do my best, with all my knowingness and experience, to describe what I have come to know as the dimensions of our human potential.

And so, from where I stand...*the Planets Align so Rare*.

Section One

The Internal Self

The perfection of any matter, the highest
or the lowest, touches the divine.
—Martin Buber

one
Our Self: the Physical Being

Remember always that you have not only the right to be an individual; you have an obligation to be one. You cannot make any useful contribution in life unless you do this.
—ELEANOR ROOSEVELT

At the moment of our birth, we look to the east and find our rising sign–the Ascendant–the imprint of the beginnings of our individuality. Astrologically, we associate beginnings, beginning of life, and one's personality with Aries, the sign of the Zodiac that kicks off the astrological wheel. Its planetary counterpart, Mars, gives this sign its dynamic energy so that these beginnings can take physical form.

This is the first opportunity bestowed upon us to express the potential of our uniqueness and individuality. We are born, or rather born *again*, unto the Earth.

We never really depart from this world, though the duration seems as fleeting as the blink of an eye in the grand infinite, yet simultaneously finite, existence of that which we are. At the moment of our physical birth, the planets of our solar system created a unique formation that will not be duplicated, for in that moment the vibration of the Universe was imprinted upon our being, and so began the process of the creation of life's experience; hence the rarity of this planetary alignment, as the planets do align so rare.

When we take our first breath, we begin to exist independently. That first breath begins a rhythmic vibration; the synaptic connections in the brain begin a greater dynamic pace of activity in unison with our breathing. These connections can also be the electromagnetic impulses that connect our humanness to the ethereal: the universal electromagnetic connection to the pulse of the Universe. We are vibrating in harmony with the universal energies and we are never separate from those energies. All things in the Universe have a vibration, and when we ourselves vibrate at that same level, as I will explain, we are one with the "Allness."

REMEMBERING OUR SELVES

When we are very young, we experience the first inklings of forming the creation of who we are. Our realities did not extend beyond our personal space and basic needs, and regardless of how small the sphere of existence may be for us at that time in our development, we are creating that reality–we just may not be entirely aware of that truth. A limited thought realm could also be true in the realities of some adults unless they progress to a more humanitarian existence and experience the understanding of the wholeness that we are, with and in each individual and our selves. Through our lives, we are never separate from one another. There is always that interconnectivity, but unfortunately we don't always remember it. This forgetfulness can lead, on a grand level, to wars, destruction, and disharmony among humanity. As a result of that forgetfulness, events such as those that transpired on September 11, 2001, are allowed to occur.

OUR NEW HOME, THE PHYSICAL BODY

As we emerge into the world, we need to accustom ourselves to our new environment. Before we entered the physical body, we existed in the spirit dimension, which, at times, can also be a dimension to our human potential once we have progressed to the point where we can tap into that part of our beings, as I will discuss in later chapters. The transition from spirit to matter can take a bit of adjusting, and some may feel, without knowing, that they are never really comfortable in their body. This sense of discomfort may eventually lead to health issues such as obesity and poorly developed muscle tone, simply never feeling or realizing that the body is a temple, which it is. It is the temple for which to house the spirit while having its earthly experience. This embodiment must be one of balance and harmony if we are to experience an existence filled with peace, satisfaction and the eventual unison with another and each other.

LOSING THE CONNECTION TO THE SPIRIT WORLD

At this very young stage of the Human experience, we are still connected to the spirit world. Have you ever observed when a newborn baby seems to stare at nothing in the distance, but appears almost as if it really were looking at something? It is! This little one is continually interacting with those in the spirit world! Those angelic beings constantly reassure him he is not alone along this journey. With the birth of my godson, Andreas, I have been reminded once again of these beatific interactions. I have come to know the truth that throughout this Human experience we are intended to receive guidance from the spirit world. Psychics and mediums give us this sanctified opportunity to once again interact with those who have gone before us; the average person possesses this quality, yet only very few have chosen to take advantage of this opportunity.

During the first few years of our development, our ethereal being has a strong connection to the spirit dimension. Some develop the imaginary friend, which, in my opinion, is a child's spirit guide. Most individuals are not taught that we have the ability to interact with the spirit world, and we are told that when we talk about imaginary friends, a.k.a. spirit guides, as children, what we see is just in our imagination. In fact, it really is our imagination; however, it's not imagination as something illusory but rather something that can be very much a part of our reality, if we are open to that possibility. Perhaps as we as a race progress in this human state of being, the children of the future will have the opportunity at home and in schools to know and learn of the spirit world as an aspect of this human experience and not something we see on TV or in the movies as being foreign or frightening. As beneficial as the media can be, it also has twisted and distorted many truths about spirit and matter into something that can be seen as sensational. Interestingly enough, the planet of grand illusion and ambiguity, Neptune, rules the spirit dimension (as we will discuss in chapter twelve). It is somewhat ironic how this planet of spirituality is also the planet of illusion and confusion. However, once the confusion has passed and the fog that Neptune creates has lifted, we are presented with great clarity and a highly refined sense of spirituality. So, because of this illusiveness of the spirit world ruled by Neptune, we often are presented with misrepresented half-truths.

RECONNECTING

We are in constant communication with our spirit guides at a young age. If we were taught to continue that communion throughout our lives, we could maintain the guidance and support of our loved ones who have gone before us, as well as, dare I say, the archangels–as high as the cherubim and the seraphim. We would always know that those who have passed before us are always with us, they are ever-present to inspire and guide us, and the Earthly grief we have come to know may not necessarily have to be as devastating as it feels. To this day, there are moments when the many souls I have known who have passed before me surprise me with signs and messages when I least expect it. When I moved into my first home, my Grandmother would playfully turn on the lamps in my bedroom late at night as I tried to drift into sleep.

During the early stages of our lives, the brain demonstrates low brainwave frequencies–alpha and theta and perhaps, at times, as low as delta–that allow us the connection to the spirit world. I'll discuss these brainwave levels in further detail in chapter three. During times of deep prayer or meditation (in truth, aren't prayer and meditation really one and the same), the brainwaves slow down, allowing us to interact with the spirit dimension and opening the doors for Divine inspiration. We come even closer during sleep. I feel that during the sleep process, we are quite possibly interacting with the spirit dimension. That may be why dreams often do not make sense. We are experiencing ourselves in a different realm. Our spirits also need a break from the heavy, dense matter of the physical being.

Psychics, mediums, and those of a high spiritual development become consciously aware of this connection. (I further discuss this topic in later chapters.) Some of us come into this dimension at a specific time and space on this plane of existence to become messengers. So, those who demonstrate psychic and mediumistic qualities are born at a moment in time when the planets align in a specific configuration manifesting the potential for these individuals to use this universal energy to develop clairvoyance. It is part of their mission—there is usually a strong influence from Neptune and the sign Pisces somewhere in the astrological composition of these individuals. Just as all of us have chosen the potential we are to demonstrate before entering the body, these entities chose to use the psychic potential of their being as part of their Human experience.

Before entering our physical existence, we each, as individuals, can choose to demonstrate these abilities once we take corporeal form. If, however, one were to have the opportunity to choose something another cannot, it would indicate that the Universe is conditional. Not all may choose to be channels to the spirit realm; it is simply not the path they have chosen and the potential they are to exhibit while in Earthly form.

The Body Beautiful

We may often wonder why we have chosen our specific and unique body before entry. If we are to look at this concept through human eyes, we may only see the physical as opposed to the beauty of the individuality of this form. This physical aspect of our being truly is the body beautiful, although most of humanity does not see that potential. The body is the suit in which we are traveling aboard our spaceship called Earth, which allows us to exist in this dimension. On any other planet or location in space, we could not exist in this physical form without some external life support means.

Every body is perfect for its particular incarnation on this planet at this point in the space-time continuum, whether it be tall, short, obese, or muscular. It is perfect, if we choose to see the perfection and potential of this body and develop the body's innate, what we would call genetic, potential: the body's potential as it has been constructed according to its DNA composition. As part of my regimen of health, balance, and nutrition, I have incorporated bodybuilding as a significant part of my everyday wellness program. I have chosen to develop my body's genetic potential and have learned not to compare myself to another. If I were to recognize and aspire to reach the genetic potential that lies in another's body rather than my own, I would set forth in pursuit of a goal I could never achieve.

The physical body is part of our identity and individuality; it separates us from any other human being. Even with twins, there is uniqueness in their planetary composition, as well as their physical bodies. There is something different in their physical composition; they are not 100% identical. The individuality of our bodies is something to be held in reverence. If we could see the sanctity of this incarnation, perhaps there would be less illness and harm inflicted upon our vessel of physical expression. We would think twice before lighting a cigarette or consuming something less than natural or ingesting chemically created substances, which we think will cure all that ails us. Would not the Divinity that created this body give us the innate ability to heal the body? (We will discuss this aspect in chapter six.) The philosophy behind chiropractic similarly emphasizes that the great power that created the body instilled within us the power to heal the body. Even when we purchase a new car we are given a manual so that we can become familiar with its operation and learn how to maintain it. Only then, with all the working parts in order, can we strive to get the optimal performance from the car. In a way, couldn't this be the same for the maintenance of our bodies? If this Earthly vehicle does not perform to its highest potential, then all the other potentials of our Earthly experience may be thwarted.

We expend so much energy comparing ourselves to others that we often miss seeing the potential we each have within. This is usually a factor in why a person may possess a low level of self-esteem. Too much misplaced energy is directed toward how we should "look." We see what is considered to be the perfect body in magazines, whether they are fashion, fitness, or even trade. Humanity constantly scrutinizes the "look" we need to exude. Why not simply go with what feels right for us as individuals and create our own personal look? And the redirected energy will go a long way in raising one's own level of self-worth. Creating our individuality and the expression of that individuality can be one of the first examples of demonstrating our human potential as it relates to the physical form.

In physical form, we're no longer simply an ethereal being, but an ethereal being in a physical body. When we think of what may be ultimate reality, we have to perceive beyond what is physical–and look to the metaphysical (beyond what is physical). However, the physical will coexist with the ethereal while we inhabit our bodies, and the ethereal will coexist with the physical, and again visa versa–an example of the spirals of the Universe.

THE BEGINNINGS OF PHYSICAL CONSCIOUSNESS

As I mentioned previously, during the early years of our development, our consciousness is still connected to the spirit world, a connection that can continue throughout our physical existence; however, we are not really taught from the start that we have this connection. Some of us learn it later on as we experience and come to understand Spirituality, both personally and as part of the collective conscious and unconscious.

We begin to lose ethereal consciousness if we are not taught to maintain that connection to the spirit world; so begins the experience of a gradual separation of the awareness of that realm. We go about our everyday activities; we begin school, progress to college, then into the workplace. Most of our energy is directed toward existing in the physical form and interaction on the human level, not spirit. Unless we are trained to do so with various tools, such as meditation, we get so tangled in the everyday "everydayness," we lose sight that we are connected in spirit. The state of meditation allows us to be on the same plane of existence as those in the spirit world–much guidance and inspiration can be experienced while operating at this level.

OUR PERSONALITY

Intrinsic experiences from past existences, called the archetypes by psychoanalyst Carl Jung and the Akashic Records by psychic Edgar Cayce, are what is carried into this incarnation and have been a part of the infinite continuum of the existence of our essence. At this early stage in the game of life, what else would we know? We haven't done much yet.

The Akashic Records can be described as a massive computer memory system, although if this were a real computer along the realm of what we understand computers to be, it would surely dwarf any possible machine rendered by humankind. This cosmic library holds all the information of the Allness, as well as every potential outcome of every probable experience. Every thought created by humanity, every experience, and every planetary configuration is recorded within this cosmic databank. In fact, any insight into the Akashic Records is insight into the nature of ourselves and our connection to the All That Is.

In addition to the containment of all things, which already may have come to pass, exists the possibility of the potentials of that which we may choose to create. Just like a computer that contains the possibilities of all the outcomes of all combinations, so, too, does this great book of records.

For example, how does a baby instinctively know to suck on its mother's breast for its nourishment? It just knows. The fears of falling and loud noises are also innate fears, but where do they come from? They emerge from the instincts. Perhaps these two innate fears originate from the memory of the spirit traveling at such great speeds through the vastness of space that, upon arrival on Earth, the sudden ending of the journey may have actually felt like falling from space. And for the fear of loud noises, perhaps the big bang startled the essence of the spirit with a fright that was encoded within that being. When we are drifting to sleep, do we not experience moments where we seem to be falling and are quickly awakened, seemingly jolted back into the body? This could very well be the spirit rushing back to the body, an experience that was associated with this fear of falling that may have been instilled within the psyche.

So then, from where would our instincts, those natural impulses that defy human logic, emanate; where do they have their origins? From the metaphysical standpoint, they can radiate from a past existence (as with a child prodigy), they can be part of the collective unconscious, or be the encoding of the divinity within us all. One aspect is not necessarily more right than the other, just a different option.

A Book Of Wonder

Again, I am not one to regularly quote from the Bible, however, I do feel there are truths in that material and, as with all things historic, they are simply the interpretation of humanness, just as the manifestation of the book you are reading is the interpretation of my human experience. There are many mentions in the Bible of a "book of records," and a passage from *The Aquarian Gospel of Jesus the Christ*, 158:3-4, states:

> And Jesus opened up to [the disciples] the meaning of the hidden way and the Holy Breath, and of the light that cannot fail. He told them all about The Book of Life, the Rolls of Graphael, the Book of God's Remembrance, where all thoughts and words of men are written down.

What is referred to as The Book of Life in this passage, as well as in the Bible, may, in fact, be interpreted as the recordings of the Akashic Records. In Revelations, The Book of Life is referenced many times. All that exists and is to exist and that which is brought to form resides in this great Universal library. We are creative beings tapping into this great cosmic encyclopedia bringing to human form the wonders that exist in the Universe–the great wonders of the Allness, the All That Is. Our human potential already lies in the Universe; we must choose to bring it to form through our humanness.

RISING IN THE EAST

Our views of the world and how the world views us would be called, in Astrological jargon, the rising sign, or the ascendant: the sign that ascends the horizon at the exact moment of our birth. For example, I have a Sagittarius rising, so I tend to see things from a philo-sophical perspective and I love fire and fireplaces–one of the many traits of Sagittarius. I am always burning can-dles as opposed to light bulbs.

We are individuals, hence we see earthly experi-ences from a different perspective; why else would we choose to come to this existence? Diversity really is something to be celebrated if we are to enjoy the full-ness of these incarnations on the Earth. We are also in creation of the world we see. If we choose to see a world of hate and anger, we create experiences sur-rounded with hateful and angry people. If we choose to see a world of beauty, balance and perfect symmetry, even amidst all that which is seemingly negative, we can create the experience of a loving, harmonious, and peaceful world.

Imprinting Our Potential

Freud believed that as we continue to grow and experience, our personalities are modified. I would tend to agree with this—if it were not true, we would remain stagnant. My dear friend Dr. Ginger describes our personalities as the sum total of our past experiences. I would include our past-life experiences, as well. I do not agree that we are incapable of changing who we are and the manner in which we react to life's experiences—this becomes possible with a consciousness and clarity of one's self.

As we move through this journey of life and as our experiences elevate us to new levels of clarity, we are able to choose our realities with a higher degree of awareness. And when we choose with greater awareness, we are able to consciously modify who we are so that our existence is congruent with our desire to express our "true" potential self. If we were to choose to observe ourselves—and this may be a challenge for some, for we do not always have the desire to see what we each consider to be less-than-perfect within ourselves nor the desire to admit that we may compare ourselves to the world's view of what may be considered perfection—and make modifications to the actions and behaviors that do not serve us, we would surely exist in a place of greater peace and happiness.

Part of the astrological imprint could be a carry-over from another time, or even all time past–there is a theory that the sign that occupies the cusp of the twelfth house, where deep subconscious memories of the past–as well as past lives–exist, could be the sign our Natal Sun occupied while in our last existence. The child prodigy who begins to demonstrate extraordinary talents at a young age–such as Mozart did with, "Andante," his first composition for keyboard that he wrote when he was just five–may have carried these talents from a previous incarnation and is still connected with his ethereal being. Again, that child was born at a precise moment in time and space so that the astrological energies could be imprinted upon the being of the physical child enabling him to use those energies in creating his individual reality.

The realization of the potential that lies within our physical form can be, for some, the first aspect of our human potential to be realized–or it may be the last. There is no linear progression to this process. Just as the ethereal being travels on what is referred to as spiral time–time that has no linear progression but is a process of evolution and progression of the essence of the being–the course through this book will be similar. Though it is intended to be experienced from beginning to end, the aspects of the realization of the human potential need not be in that order.

WE BEGIN, AND WE BEGIN AGAIN

As mentioned at the start of this chapter, beginnings in the astrological realm associate themselves with the zodiac sign Aries and the planet of dynamic energy, Mars. This energy can be seen as the spark that ignites the flames of fire, which suggests ambition and desire. In order for anything to "begin," there needs to be a combustion, the coming together of dynamic, individual energies–such a the union of a sperm and egg to create the physical form–so that all other energies and manifestations will follow. Another biblical notation reads, "...for wherever two or more of you are gathered, so there shall I be..." This describes a coming together of energies so that potential may be realized. Another definition for the entity we call God may be that God is the absoluteness of human potential.

The physical body is the vehicle for which the etheric being travels upon this Earth spacecraft and is the first aspect of the human potential in this discussion, which we may realize and elaborate upon. The genetic potential of this physical form is unique and specific to the individual, which allows us to celebrate the diversity of this uniqueness, if we so choose.

two

Self-worth and Abundance

*Every man has to seek his own way to
make his own self more noble and to
realize his own worth.*
—Albert Schweitzer

As we become increasingly aware of the reality in which we exist in this human form and the way we continually create our realities becomes more and more apparent to us, particularly after arriving at a place where that reality has been brought to form with awareness, we begin to see beyond our personal sphere of existence and establish within ourselves a sense of self-worth as we craft and modify the distinctness of who we are.

Again, remember that this process is not necessarily a linear progression from birth to adulthood and then to the transition from this plane of existence to the next; it can be experienced at any time during our Earthly experience when we choose to have the experience. For many, this quality is measured by our relationship to that which is external, which, in truth, does not give accurate measure to the full potential of one's worth. We will often find our self to be substandard when measured against something external. The attribute of self-worth must confidently radiate from within and move out toward the external.

On the astrological level, the sign of the zodiac Taurus associates itself with our material possessions, that which brings us security through material posses-sions, wealth and the creature comforts, and the adorn-ments we all desire. Taurus' planetary complement, Venus, adds beauty and charm to those embellish-ments. Venus shines like a diamond in the sky during the early morning hours. She is the ruler of songs and sonnets, silk and satin–just to name a few of her crea-ture comforts. Venus is all things beautiful, and in those things we include the self and the beautification of the self and our surroundings. (In astrological terms, Venus rules the Earth, so it's not coincidental that she is also known as the Earth's twin.) As there is an innate, natu-ral beauty that exists in nature, so does this natural beauty exist within the self and the external objects with which we surround ourselves.

FINDING SELF-WORTH

As we become more aware that we are existing in a physical world, we begin to progress beyond the physical self. Our desires grow toward creating a surrounding existence filled with things of beauty; physical things outside of the body ascertain a sense of importance and, for some, the amount of the accumulation of those things can measure our social status, instill a sense of success and perhaps provide a barometer to measure how much we have achieved and progressed while on Earth. These external things can radiate from our personal sense of self-worth as a reflection of our personalities. However, there may be moments during the realization of the human potential when we create profusely, yet the feeling of our worth may not necessarily be in congruence with the abundance of the material possessions. Someone with great material wealth may have created that wealth in order to compensate for a lack of self-worth. And one with a seemingly great sense of self-worth may be experiencing a life of living simply. The external experience may not necessarily be an accurate representation of an individual's sense of self-worth.

A TRUTH ABOUT MATERIAL POSSESSIONS

During our progression through life, we become aware of a personal space, our own sphere of reality where whatever composes that space is sacred to our existence: the personal "Sacred Space." I will discuss how the physical home is our Sacred Space in chapter four. This part of our discussion is dedicated to the creation of the material things outside the physical body and how they, in part, reflect one's self-worth. In this instance, self-worth can also be viewed as a personal validation of the self.

Our personalities that progress through this life strive for our own sense of personal security. Because here on the Earth plane we live in the world of the physical and the relative (as opposed to the world of the absolute, which is the spirit realm), during this experience we may not always demonstrate a highly evolved sense of being when it comes to the material aspect of our experience. If we did, we would come upon the knowledge that all we truly need is the air we breathe. (There are those who exist who are known as Breatherians–beings who do not eat, but rather draw nourishment directly from the atmosphere in which they are placed. I personally would not suggest this form of behavioral discipline; however, there are those who choose to do so and stand as examples that we can exist on Earth simply by breathing the air.)

Because there are moments when we forget our connection to the All That Is and that we are one with that Allness, we feel the need to create those external things as our security blankets–the creature comforts, wealth and the like. Let me clarify from the beginning: there is nothing intrinsically wrong with creating great material wealth and surrounding ourselves with adornments and the wondrous things we consider necessary so that we may reside in a snug environment. What may be of disservice to our being, and humanity, is the false idolatry that may be placed on those objects, be it money, gold, property, whatever those secular things may be. In today's society, these material possessions seem to be a reflection of one's self-worth; however, it may not necessarily be an accurate reflection. At times, it may be a mask. I feel we all are worthy of abundance; it is our choice if we will make it real.

The disservice I mentioned refers to one having the "need" of those material things, meaning that one's existence would be thwarted if a certain lack of material or physical possession were to occur. The mask I refer to is when we create a tremendous amount of material possessions because we sometimes, unknowingly, sense there is a lack of some quality within ourselves. We create the external abundance thinking this will compensate for the deficiency.

If we were to take the time to review the origins of this sensation, we may see our reality with different eyes. An axiom in the Bible states: "It is easier for a camel to pass through the eye of a needle than a rich man to enter into the kingdom of Heaven." I understand this passage to mean that we really need nothing of and from the physical world once we depart from it, so collecting material wealth and hording it is as pointless as trying to thread a needle with a camel. You can't take it with you. We truly can exist with very little if there is a necessity to do so, and yet it is also okay to have it all. And it's cool to have it and enjoy it while we are here on Earth. What we must evaluate is the value we ascribe to those material things, and we must remember not to place false idolatry on those possessions. They are only manifestations of the Earth and physical being, and like all things on this Earth and through this experience, they are temporary.

I believe this was the original and true meaning of the second Holy Commandment listed in the Bible. Regardless of religious beliefs, to cherish material possessions over one's own physical and spiritual being, as well as over other people, can only lead that person to a life of avaricious emptiness. Life becomes flat and meaningless when one covets "stuff" so much that he not only fears sharing his possessions, he stops sharing himself with the All That Is. Only a barren existence can result.

When we finally understand that all that is necessary for our existence is already within the self, the "need" for the external may become insignificant. Again, I understand we are in the physical world and there is a seeming necessity for all Earthly things; however, I am here to explain we have the ability, if the necessity arose, to exist without the physical accoutrements. Think of the lyrics to the Hollies' song: "All I need is the air that I breathe."

TRUST VS. MISTRUST

In psychoanalyst Erik Erikson's theory of self-development, the first stage in our development upon which all other levels are built deals with the manner in which our trust issues are established very early during our Earthly experience. Simply stated, we either learn to trust another individual or we progress through life's experiences doubting the genuine qualities of another, which also may be transformed into a lack of self-worth and ultimately becomes a false representation of who we are. We find ourselves moving forward with a sense of caution, which may lead to a debilitation of action. Consequently, we limit that which we allow ourselves to experience and, to the potential extreme, do nothing at all.

Another aspect of this potential is that we create a tremendous amount of material wealth and success and we choose to harbor all that is great and good in our lives for ourselves, feeling that if we share too much or too often, someone will take away something from our self that we have strived so meticulously to create. Of course, we may conduct ourselves in this manner, either consciously or unconsciously–regardless, the choice is always ours.

Trust can be one of the most significant traits we establish as a young child. It can define the way we relate to one another throughout the course of our existence and contribute to the classification of our personal self-worth.

Creating a Trust in Abundance

The condition of the lack of trust of others can emanate from a lack of trust within the self. In this human form, we are mirrors of each other representing the physical manifestation of something that dwells deep within the fabric of the self. The manifestation of those traits reflected in another allows us to see something within ourselves of which we may not have awareness. This is likely something we would prefer to overlook, for those inferior qualities we readily observe in another are usually the same qualities we are not so quick to acknowledge might exist within ourselves. We simply dismiss them as just being something we do not like about another. However, if we were to choose to see these situations as opportunities to review and evaluate something inside the self that may not necessarily be obvious without the interaction of another, this opportunity would afford us the ability to change that part of the self that may be less than humanitarian.

Yes, it can be a truth that in this dimension of existence there are those individuals who are not trustworthy, who will spare no expense regardless of the costs another may incur so that they may rise to their own occasion, and who exist only as self-serving. I am not suggesting that we blindly walk through this life and lessen that trust quality; I am proposing that we act with awareness about the qualities within the self, in this case, the issues of trust. If we act with a sense of unshakeable trust within our selves, we will be drawn to those individuals with similar qualities, allowing us the opportunity to interact with others who possess a sense of trust similar to that which we hold within our selves.

The mirror in another will reflect back to us those qualities we demonstrate within the self, allowing us to attract another with comparable quality.

If we move through this existence not trusting, seeing humanity as deceitful, calculating and conniving, manipulating and shrewd, we will create those situations where we will attract individuals radiating those qualities. On the plane of the collective unconscious, we do the same with our government, political, and spiritual leaders. That which exists in our dimension of reality, exists somewhere in the fabric of our being; the behavioral manifestations of others reflect what is within the self. At the collective level, we can observe how these issues of trust, as well as other qualities we will review, radiate from the essence of the self, along the etheric continuum of the Earth, throughout humanity.

As humankind progresses to a higher level of evolution, there will undoubtedly be a shift in the qualities of those who represent humanity on the global scale in terms of politics and religion that will transform into spirituality as we progress closer to the Age of Aquarius. As we exist as individuals and allow a shift in and of our own consciousness to take root within the structure of the being, this energy will radiate to the masses. Again, like the ripples on a pond created by the cast of a stone, when the shift of consciousness takes place first and foremost within and of the self, these qualities will radiate to the whole of humanity.

THE CREATURE COMFORTS

We are discussing the aspect of our human potential where we create security through wealth and material possessions. I have come to know that the accumulation of wealth, success, abundance and prosperity is part of our birthright–as with all aspects of our human potential, we must choose it to be so. However, for the most part this truth is not something instilled within us. We have come to Earth to live, love, invent, reinvent and experience ourselves as creative beings in and with abundance and prosperity. Some may have chosen to come to the Earth plane to experience themselves through what may be construed as a "lack" of the most basic of human requirements, but it does not necessarily have to be experienced in this manner. However, the accumulation of great wealth need not be a measure of the evolution of one's self, either. Mother Theresa lived what we would call a life of poverty; however, through that experience she may have come to know herself as creative and divine. Poverty was the path she chose to experience her divinity. It is all a part of the mysticism of that which we are; we simply need to choose it to be so regardless of what the creation may be.

Some of the ideologies concerning wealth may have been instilled within each of us, as most of the "programs" that may decree our behaviors are set in place while we are still very young. If we were to review our thoughts about money and material possessions, we could see exactly how we have created the condition in which we exist regarding money and wealth. The same holds true for any other condition, for that matter. We will discuss this topic in greater detail in the following chapter as we review the creation of reality through our thought process.

THE LAW OF CAUSE AND EFFECT

What goes around comes around; what we send out to the Universe, in terms of the vibration that radiates from our being along the ether, will be returned to us one-hundredfold. The beauty of the simplicity of this truth is something I feel has been lost, or more accurately forgotten, by humanity. If not, we would think twice about some of the things we say and do to one another. In other words, do unto others as you would have done unto you! How simple, yet so easily forgotten, is this truth.

How many times have we heard something like "Give freely and it will be returned to you one-hundredfold." This is a great truth that would serve humanity well if we were to incorporate this understanding into our existence. If we were to demonstrate this truth, would not our generosity be that much more abundant knowing our bounteousness will be returned to us? Perhaps there would be less global deficit and more global abundance. There would not exist the feeling that one nation can lose something to another; rather, in the sharing of our abundance with each other, we give to each other opportunity and prosperity.

This is such a simple and great truth. The Universe does not assign a prosperous experience to one and adversity to another. Some may disagree, but I have come to know this as truth-perhaps just my truth, but truth nonetheless. Why would some live an existence filled with a multitude of adornments, exorbitances and what might seem to be unnecessary luxuries, and some live a life of hapless poverty? If the Universe were to grant this to one individual and not another, this would suggest that the Universe is conditional. Yet, it is not. If a condition is true for one, the same condition must be true for another. It is the individual being who chooses the kind of life he will experience, and the individuality of that expression is what is unique to the personality.

THE BIG PICTURE

Self-worth as an aspect of the human potential can be defined as the "self" (the true essence of what we are) knowing its "worth" (the full potential of what is within the self). This aspect is in a sense all encompassing because even though all dimensions of the human potential can radiate to all areas of our life, the sense of self-worth is what gives substance to each of those dimensions and how they are manifested.

As we advance with awareness from the physical self, discussed in the first chapter, we come to desire material things, those things of beauty that are of the physical world. The zodiac sign Taurus oversees the acquisition of material, and its ruler Venus–the planet of beauty and bliss, wealth and things of adornment, gifts and the luxurious–brings these worldly possessions into our lives.

As we encompass this human experience, it is the desire of the Universe for each individual, regardless of its physical manifestation (race, religion, class), to have the opportunity to experience an existence of prosperity, wealth, and abundance. It is the choice of the individual how these qualities will manifest the continuation of reality. There are those who may have embarked upon this journey we call life, choosing prior to their Earthly arrival that they would experience a life of meager means and material possessions. Perhaps they desired to experience a life of servitude to humanity. Or perhaps they desired to experience the struggle of a wanting life. That is their choice. Here I exemplify our ability to create these great possessions in accordance with the sense of self-worth within each individual.

When there exists a diminished view of the self from within, or one believes the "self" is inherently lacking in some capacity, this erroneous opinion of the self radiates throughout all other aspects of one's life. Famous author and psychologist M. Scott Peck once wrote: "Until you value yourself, you won't value your time. Until you value your time, you will not do anything with it." We have been created through and with divine intervention, as well as in co-creation with the self from all things of beauty (our dear friend Venus) and wonder, and when we come to know the true worth of the self, we can then radiate these qualities to our surrounding existence, and from there to all those on the collective realm.

May we share and share alike, knowing abundance is within, the Universe will provide, we will always have enough to go around, and, of course, what goes around will come around.

three
Thoughts

*We write our own destiny...
we become what we do.*
—MADAME CHIANG KAI-SHEK

The very inkling of the beginning of a thought is the first step on the journey to creating one's personal reality and ultimately, on a global scale, creating the condition of our planet and how we as humans co-exist with one another through the collective unconscious and its creation.

This dimension of the human potential associates itself with Mercury, the planet that represents our thoughts, the thought process, all means of communication, and the beginnings of creativity. The first planet in our solar system is named for the Messenger of the

Gods, and the sign of the zodiac over which it has dominion is Gemini, the sign of great creativity through thoughts and words. (Mercury co-rules Virgo, which we will discuss in chapter six.) However, Gemini's creative talents are sometimes incoherent or disordered. Unless the planet Mercury is well-aspected in one's chart, bringing method and order to the chaos, Gemini's thought process can lean toward the vague, and is often described as airy-fairy and ambiguous, but that is just the manner in which Gemini exudes its creativity. Gemini knows exactly what it's talking about and leaves everyone else to fend for themselves when it comes to deciphering his riddles. My natal Sun is almost in Gemini and I have a few planets in this lighthearted and vivacious sign, so my friends and family have firsthand knowledge of these characteristics of the third sign of the zodiac and how they manifest.

CREATING REALITY FROM THOUGHT

The Roman Emperor Marcus Aurelius, one of the few philosopher-kings in the history of the world, believed that "our life is what our thoughts make it." Most of us (humanity) are not educated early enough in the human experience to pay close attention to our individual thoughts at any given moment on any given day. If we did, we would comprehend exactly how our realities are created from our thoughts and thought process.

These bits of reality can vary from the simplest of

actions, such as forgetting to set an alarm clock (an unconscious act that can set into motion a new series of realities that might not have occurred if the sleeper had awakened at the desired time) to those vastly complicated thought processes such as choosing a college or, dare I say, creating a life-altering illness. This extreme is most often created, quite simply, without awareness. A person doesn't wake up one day and say to himself, "Today I choose to create cancer in my body." One small thought recited once in the mind will not instantly manifest as reality; this process comes to fruition over a period of time when the same thought is repeated over and over again in the mind, usually unconsciously at first, but then passed on to the spoken word.

The method of creating our realities so that they are in congruence with our desires can be such a simple process. But when we take on human form, we seem to forget how uncomplicated and effortless the process of creation and the power of thought and word are. If we are to choose to change the reality in which we live, we must first and foremost change our thoughts. To continue to demonstrate the same thought process while expecting the results to change is, at best, foolish, and, at worst, insane. In other words, as the saying goes, "when you do what you've always done, you get what you always got." A wonderful, short book that specifically discusses this matter is *Who Moved My Cheese* by Dr. Spencer Johnson.

A thought, notion, or idea, which are essentially all the

same, is where the beginnings of the creation and culti-
vation of our realities originate. We may dismiss these
thoughts if they don't fit in our realities for whatever reason, or we may choose to nurture these seedlings if they
are in accordance with our desires. At times, they may
not be congruent with our desire and we haphazardly
nurture those thoughts, perhaps even without an awareness of the process of creation. When we allow the creation of our reality to be dictated by uncontrolled,
unconscious thought, we experience a reality we do not
desire. It is created haphazardly without positive direction of a conscious thought. But regardless of the intent,
these seeds of thought are the dimensions of the potential of the beginning of the creation of our realities.

As I have stated, everything in the Universe possesses
a vibration. Different vibrations of light produce the different colors of the spectrum–albeit, visible or invisi-
ble–just as different frequencies produce audible and
inaudible sound vibrations. Each nerve cell in the body
has the potential to possess a certain amount of stored
electrical energy–a form of a vibration. The major function of the neurons in the body is to send information
throughout the body via an electrical pulse. This information, essentially our thoughts, radiates throughout
the body literally altering the composition of the cells of
the body and encoding each and every cell of the body
with that particular thought! (This has been scientifical-
ly proven, and for those who would like more clarity on

the subject, I suggest watching the movie *What the Bleep Do We Know!?* This movie illustrates something I have been predicting for quite some time: the growing trend toward the unification of science and spirituality.) Then, through osmosis, the framework of those thoughts is transferred from the body to our external realities via the electromagnetic pulses of the Earth's vibration.

I recall a bumper sticker I used to see when I was younger that stated "Think Snow!" Being an avid skier and having had the opportunity to ski many mountains including the wondrous Alps of Austria–I truly believe that in Austria, all they do is think snow–I have always loved that bumper sticker and the thought of snow-covered mountains. What this bumper sticker suggested was that when enough people get together and think of snow, the thought will manifest, it will snow, and we can go skiing.

There was another bumper sticker in the late '80's, which I sported on my own car, that read "Visualize World Peace." This truth about creating reality has been around for an infinite number of years; it's time we pay meticulous attention to our creation of thought so we can produce positive realities that will benefit and enlighten humanity and will be revealed more profoundly in the coming years.

TWO DIMENSIONS OF THE THOUGHT POTENTIAL

Two types of thoughts steer our behavior: negative thoughts and positive thoughts, similar to the negative and positive charge of a battery–in fact, it's not much different on the Metaphysical scale. Positive thoughts are "light" and inspiring while the negative thoughts are "dark" and toxic and can quite literally weigh us down. For some reason, we are prone to the drama of possessing negative thoughts, and the "thought" of maintaining a positive mind frame seems to have escaped the realm of our early development.

The majority of humanity is programmed to lean toward the negative. We become so engulfed within those thoughts that we are not aware what it is we are creating in our realities. In fact, many people learn that when they exhibit any negative drama, they receive attention from others. Like a moth to a flame, we are drawn to negativity or some negative occurrence.

Let me use this semi-fictional example of a woman–I'll call her Shelley–who has seemingly unconsciously created a life-challenging situation through a terminal illness. This is not to say that everyone who suffers this type of life-altering disease has created the situation I am about to illustrate in this exact manner, and by no means do I intend to lessen any challenge created in one's life due to an unimaginable ailment.

Over the course of many years, I would hear sad tales from Shelley (for the purpose of this story, I'll say she is now in her mid-40's), who lives with a terminal illness. Throughout her life, she would engage in reckless, self-destructive activities many people would regard as negative, such as the consumption of intoxicating amounts of drugs and alcohol, and participation in frequent, indiscriminate sex. Because she lacked awareness and understanding of her true self and feared confronting the truth behind her poor self-image, Shelley chose to engage in negative and self-destructive behavior. Because of the aforementioned behavior, she created dramatic situations in her life, both conscious and unconscious, that included car accidents, hospital stays, broken bones, and drug rehab. The creation of these situations also created a "woe is me" attitude. "Look at all these horrific things happening to me. Give me attention!"

The creation of this behavior progressed over the course of her life, from a minor scraped knee as a clumsy child to a major car accident as an adult, and it even may have originated from an event in her early childhood that was mistaken as insignificant. This process has led Shelley to learn that negative conditions in her life would bring her the attention she desired, or even needed.

Of course, at any moment, when Shelley encounters anyone, whether it is while walking through the mall, or receiving a call from a caring friend, these tales of woe are passed on to the unsuspecting bystander. By continually telling these tales of difficulty and despair, she is enforcing her negativity and passing it on to others, and probably doing so unwittingly. This transference of negative energy from one person to another can continue unceasingly, much like a communicable disease–which, in actuality, is a manifestation of extreme negative and toxic energy.

Again, it is not my intention to diminish the experience anyone endures under such horrifying circumstances as a terminal disease: however, there comes a time when we must summon the strength from within to overcome any obstacle, regardless of the challenge. Just about everyone has heard a story of a person who one day made a decision to stop being a victim of their "hard luck" and stood up to the challenge before them. The person made a choice to overcome their heartache and turn their life from a negative to a positive. It can sometimes seem, especially when the hardship is a terminal disease, that the person has achieved the impossible or that a miracle occurred. It wasn't impossible or a miracle, in the fantastical sense, but rather a person's human potential to summon the strength to overcome any obstacle–an ability innate in all of us.

These negative dramatists begin to thrive on this attention, thus the vicious cycle of negativity begins. We are all guilty of this at one time or another. We direct the attention of others toward ourselves, and this allows us to thrive on the negative energy we radiate. So, without consciousness, we have created an experience that is not beneficial to the existence of the self and, in the process, radiated negative energy to others, as illustrated in the above example.

When we convey to another the smallest nicety, do we not in and through ourselves feel lighter? It feels so satisfying to compliment another, and it's so easy to do; yet for some, it may seem a most difficult task.

When we are in the company of one who exudes nothing but negativity, we can literally feel that person's negative energy. If one is not aware of the energy force surrounding a negative person or experience, that energy can easily transfer itself from the negative person to another and then manifest within the new host. A negative person can be a "Succubus" of another's life force. The negative energy, which originated from that first negative individual's thought process and which created negative experiences in that same negative individual's life, has now been transferred to another. The result: we get slimed with negative psychic ectoplasm. If you have ever been in the presence of one who is toxically negative, then walk away from that experience and feel the heaviness that fills your spirit, you will know exactly what I am referring to. You've been psychically slimed!

"AS A MAN THINKETH"

"As a man thinketh in his heart, so he is," from James Allen's very tiny, yet influential book *As a Man Thinketh*, simply illustrates the notion that the composition of our thoughts will create the reality in which we live.

Included in this process of the creation of our realities is the spoken word. Just as our thoughts create our reality, so do the words we speak as we attempt to describe the thoughts that dance in our minds. This process of creating personal reality manifests itself through thoughts, then words, then our actions. Thoughts alone, in and of themselves, do not manifest the physical reality; the spoken word becomes the next step in the creative process of the demonstration of our realities. This is a component of the creative process; the thought process is the first. When we discover ourselves "walking the walk and talking the talk," we will manifest a reality that is consistent with our innermost desires.

RELAX, AND THEN GO WITHIN

Creative thinking originates from deep within the mental process. A great man named Jose Silva, who developed the Silva Method of Mental Dynamics, discovered that the optimal brainwave frequency for creative thinking and problem solving is the brainwave frequency that repeats at 10-cycles per second. A brainwave is defined in Webster's II as "a rhythmic fluctuation of electric potential between parts of the brain." Electric potential is the essence of the capability and possibility of a thought. Depending on the experience at hand, these "waves" will operate at various frequencies throughout our existence.

The four dimensions of the brainwave potential are Delta, Theta, Alpha, and Beta. While we operate in the physical world (the "awake" part of our daily experience, the outer conscious level), we are functioning at the Beta level of the brainwave frequency. These vibrations are on a scale from zero (almost nonexistent) to as high as 21 and greater (the waking state). The center of the Beta scale is approximately 21 cycles (vibrations) per second, or "cps," and the center of the Alpha level is about 10 cps.

The Alpha level is where dreams exist; it is also part of the spirit dimension and our inner conscious level. The center of any given thing is where its strongest potential will exist; hence the central frequency of the Alpha brainwave potential is at 10 cps. When we are in a dream state, either day or night, the brain emanates a vibration of 10 cps; the same holds true during meditation and prayer. These are the levels of optimum creativity in the thought process. It is here where we are free from worldly distraction and where we can communicate and commune with the Divine and receive inspiration. (We will discuss Inspiration as Divine intervention in chapter nine.)

How many stories have been told of individuals who wake up in the middle of the night with thoughts and ideas of grand proportion and great potential? Could it be that during sleep we have been in communion with the spirit dimension, receiving direction and insight into what may benefit us as individuals, as well as greater humanity? We hear of many songwriters who woke during the night to the sound of great musical compositions playing in their mind. Billy Joel has described this as the divine intervention for his song *River of Dreams*.

> In the middle of the night
> I go walking in my sleep
> From the mountains of faith
> To the river so deep.

THE COMMUNION OF THOUGHT AND COMMUNICATION

Many years ago, I learned that in order to maintain a congruency between my "self" and the outside world, it would serve me well to "say what I mean and mean what I say." This truth demonstrates the congruency, or lack thereof, between one's thoughts and the spoken word.

Words are the verbal expression of our thoughts. They are thoughts manifesting themselves in form and are the second part of the creation of our realities (thoughts are the first). Words are one aspect in which we convey to one another meanings of the self and what we represent. Words, at times, may seem limiting when expressing the true self. We do, in fact, use other forms of communication, which I will describe, but the simplest and most obvious manner in which we express ourselves is through the spoken word.

When inconsistencies in communication–incongruities between our thoughts, our words, and our actions–are allowed to run amok during the course of existence, we are faced with a reality that may not meet our true intentions. These inconsistencies may result from a lack of understanding of either the true nature of the self or that which we truly desire. Or perhaps the incongruity occurs because we choose not to express the truth of our desires, but instead choose to colorfully express ourselves in a manner not congruent with the internal self.

Why do these incongruities manifest themselves? At times it may be an unintentional or an unconscious action. We simply speak without giving much thought to what we are saying. It's much easier to just speak without carefully choosing our words than to make an honest attempt at saying exactly what it is we mean. What purpose does it serve to say something if we really have no meaning behind it?

For example, without realizing the influential effects the words we speak have on the creation of our realities, we may foolishly declare as we leave our homes to go to our offices every morning, "Here I go back to that miserable place again!" First of all, without realizing the power and impact of our words, we are unaware that we are, in fact, creating the workplace as being something miserable. The creation of this reality will come to pass over time if every morning we leave our homes and make this statement until it becomes embedded in our minds. It eventually is transferred out to the ether of the Earth where the thought manifests to reality.

The first time these words were innocently spoken may have been a result of the prior day filled with unpleasant events that made a significant impression on the individual. The statement was verbalized once, without conscious recognition of the statement, only to become a daily mantra, repeated over and over again. If, in fact, that individual were to review the events of that discontented day and described them more accurately, with awareness, perhaps a different course of events would come to pass. The day may have been one of abundant strain and stress (a culmination of energies in and of itself) perhaps not accurately representing the true nature of that workplace, but rather a misconception of an isolated event now lodged in the person's mind, forever changing the views of that workplace.

At times, we may also observe that what we are expressing really is not something from the self, but something we think others may want to hear. Or maybe some random thought has been programmed inside the mind and we have become so accustomed to this thought that we do not bother to think about what we are saying. How many times do we sacrifice the self in order to please another so that we may "fit in," or perhaps we simply choose to do so to avoid rejection–as may be the case in a lover-type relationship? We say what we think the other wants to hear to avoid conflict or rejection from the other. These inconsistencies lead to imbalance over a long period of time between the internal and external self. Eventually, we no longer can keep up the charade, so we find ourselves distraught or even resentful of the situation.

This is essentially anger towards the self, for deep

inside lies the understanding that we are not being truthful in the expression of the self. We may choose to blame another, but, in fact, if we carefully review what we have done, we'll often find that the fault lies in the inconsistencies between what we feel or believe and what we actually communicate to another.

TYPES OF COMMUNICATION

We, as humans, express ourselves by utilizing various tools of communication. The spoken word is the most obvious; however, there are other manners in which we convey our perceptions, opinions, and ideas. Some may be obvious, while others may be hidden, subtle. Though the concept of oral communication may seem straight-forward, local culture can have an enormous impact on a people's common language when conveying one's thoughts through spoken word.

The posture of the body and the physical expression of the self also convey our thoughts and emotions in subtle ways, yet the behavior is obvious when we observe with awareness the physical messages of another. This is called "non-verbal communication." For example, a person may say "Yes, I am telling you the truth" while shaking his head from side to side. This indicates a clear discrepancy in the intended communication. He is verbally stating "Yes" while his true intention is "No." The individual is non-verbally saying no while he is orally stating yes. This is a very simple example; the complexity of these forms of communication would require a volume of books.

One New Age school of thought that can be used to understand the various ways in which we communicate is Neuro Linguistic Programming (NLP), the manner in which we communicate with ourselves and with others. NLP helps one to understand how we receive information and how we disperse information. We learn what affects both our behavior and the responses we receive from others by understanding inconsistencies within the self and in the manner in which those inconsistencies are expressed.

We communicate aurally by the way we "listen," as well as "hear." Has anyone ever said to you, "I know you are talking, but all I hear is *blah blah blah...*"? This exemplifies someone who is not listening as well as he can hear. (Or, perhaps, you are not saying what you mean and, in this process, confusing the person to whom you are speaking.) During a physical two-way conversation (I say physical because in this instance there are two or more individuals demonstrating the action of communication but not really saying anything or hearing what the other is expressing), one individual is making an attempt at conveying what she is trying to say while the other is mentally thinking about what he will say next. This second individual is hearing but not listening to what the first individual is saying. By doing this, the second individual is aurally demonstrating that he really doesn't care about what the other is saying. This will affect the dynamics of the communication process and the dynamics of the conversation.

Of course, this can also be true in a converse circumstance. Perhaps the first person makes a statement, but that statement doesn't jibe with his actions or expressions. Then it stands to reason that the second person in the conversation will not understand the first. The first person isn't being honest in his verbal communication, or perhaps isn't fully thinking through his thought process before making his statement. It's as important to speak thoughtfully as it is to listen thoughtfully.

Another type of communication, Responsive Communication, describes one's ability to listen and understand as a basis in which we respond to others.

When our intent is to truly listen to another, to understand the thoughts beneath the conveyed words and behavior, we find ourselves becoming respectful, more humble, in how we respond to the individual. When we learn to "listen [to] as well as we hear" (as stated in the 1989 song by Mike and the Mechanics' *The Living Years*) the true meaning of what is being conveyed to us by employing love, understanding, and humility–minus the ego–we become more gentle and loving in our response to one another. When we recognize that someone is approaching us out of anger, if we respond with love, the situation will certainly diffuse, moving in an alternate direction than if we acted on the defensive.

INTERPERSONAL COMMUNICATION

Communication is the most basic means of interaction with others and yet it seems to be the area in our lives where we are most challenged when we are interacting with another. It seems that the culprit of most failed relationships is lack of communication, as well as communication that inaccurately represents who we are.

The first experience of interactive communication is more than likely with one's parents. When we are very young, there is limited interaction with the outside world. Yes, there are other relatives who we are in contact with, other young individuals we intermingle with when we go out to play. But the majority of the initial interactions are with the parents. They truly are our first educators, particularly in how we learn to communicate with others.

During these early stages, everything we observe becomes instilled within us. These are the subtle programs that dictate behavior, and unless there is an understanding of the behavior patterns, we will continue to demonstrate those patterns throughout the life experience. If the manner of communication we exhibit is less than we would desire, there must take place a conscious effort to change that behavior or we will continue to exhibit those same behaviors for eternity, or at least this life's experience.

When a child begins to observe that it's not just "me" as he interacts and communicates with his siblings (with an only child, this awareness will come while interacting with children outside the immediate family and relatives or their early friendships), this epiphany that the Universe does not revolve around him can be a rude awakening for him! In fact, there are some adults who would be wise to come to that realization, as well. We reside in a place where we must understand the dynamics of co-existing with another human. These early realizations can dictate how the means of communication establish themselves, and the individual's persona plays a part. Personality, as described in chapter one, plays a large part in how one expresses oneself in terms of communication, and one of the first opportunities to do so is with brothers and sisters. In my case, it was, in addition to my biological brother, my cousins who filled those roles.

Continuing along the progression of life, we begin to interact with the outside world and establish relation-ships that progress to friendships–another opportunity for the individual to discover his personal manner of communication. In the dynamics of this interaction, we may discover that the way in which we express our-selves may be different than we do with our parents. We may find that during this instance we are freer to express our true self. We may not feel the pressure to do or say what is the right thing to say; we may discover our true means and freedom of expression with these rela-tionships. Not to say this is without boundary or disci-pline, for in those formative years there is a definite need of direction; however, this may be the first taste one is given to experience self-expression without fear of disapproval or disappointment from an elder.

As we grow older still during this journey of life, we desire the companionship and camaraderie of someone who fills a role greater in depth than that of a platonic friendship, and so we choose the expression of the inter-action with a spouse or life partner. The communication dynamic in these relations can deviate dramatically from those of other forms of interaction. It seems we are very quick to use vulgar and less-than-loving words of commu-nication with the one whom we consider our beloved, especially if they are not in agreement with our desires. It always seems we so easily choose to hurt the ones we love with harsh words. The communication in this instance can be one of great love and devotion for we may find that in these relationships we are most vulner-able and free to articulate the most intimate of expres-sions. If there has been established a great sense of trust in this relationship, we are free to express that part of ourselves where we may feel the most vulnerable. This is the greatest difference in this manner of communication as opposed to the form of expression with another in which we do not feel we have a profound bond.

In the workplace, we are presented with a whole new challenging dimension of communication. We share our work space, and a significant portion of our lives, with souls who do not fill a romantic or sometimes even friendship role in our lives. Because of that, we may find ourselves guarded in our method of expression for fear that another may steal our work ideas or downplay our job performance for their personal gain.

I believe that if we choose to attract a workplace filled with light, as well as a heightened sense of spirituality (which will come to pass in future years here on Earth), these reservations should be of no concern. Those who dwell in highly evolved cultures are not concerned about others stealing the uniqueness of their ideas and being used as a scapegoat to improve another's position. They understand this and thus put their faith in the win/win situation, knowing the other resides, as well, in a place of higher understanding and that the other, in that advanced place, would certainly do unto others as he would want others to do unto him. There would not be a need for guarded communication, but rather free expression without fear.

For us, as a society, to achieve this highly evolved workspace, one of light and respect, it begins with the actions of one person. And as with all positive reality, it begins with a positive thought.

CRAZINESS AND DEPRESSION

Of course, I use "craziness" in tongue-in-cheek fashion. There are those moments during the course of the human experience where there exists an extreme overcharge of excess mental thought energy that has not been channeled productively. This can result in unusual behaviors or even the more extreme psychosis.

When the mind is permitted to run amok, to wander and meander on a reckless course of endangerment, devoid of usefulness and productivity, the results can be an existence of discord and disharmony. Those who have "lost their mind" or are "out of their mind," experience the thought process in a non-productive, extreme way.

Mental illness is not something to be taken lightly nor am I posing as a psychoanalyst to diagnose mental disorder, for that would require yet another extensive volume and studies that far surpass my level of expertise. I offer another means of understanding this somewhat less than perfect quality of existence.

Some of the most brilliant men are said to have what we would consider a mental illness. Howard Hughes and even Albert Einstein could be placed in this category.

THE COLLECTIVE CREATION OF REALITY

So, if our personal thoughts on a small scale will create the sphere of our personal realities, would it not hold true that the collection of a mass quantity of personal thoughts, which would be known as the collective unconscious, create our realities on a global scale? This notion is something I will elaborate upon when I discuss the higher octave of the creative thought process in chapter nine. This allusion was suggested to tantalize and to whet your appetite!

CREATING YOUR REALITY

Every day, we have the availability, with awareness, to create the reality exactly as we so desire–if we have the understanding and clarity of what it is we truly desire–through the process of thought. This must be orchestrated with awareness at first, then with discipline and determination. A retraining of the mind's thought process must be completed in order to do so, and this must be a choice made within the individual if it's to be successful.

Mercury, who we have come to know as the Messenger of the Gods, holds court over thoughts and the thought process. The sign Gemini creatively formulates thoughts in the process of creating things or reality.

Once cognizant of the thought process as it relates to the existence and creation of humanity, we achieve greater understanding of how the realities in which we live have been created on both the personal and global scale. So, as Marcus Aurelius suggested, life truly does become what our thoughts make it.

four

Foundations

Foundation is the essence of vigor and power that resonates from within the self; simply, it is our inner strength. Foundation is the manifesto upon which we build anything in our lives. It is the confidence within the self, being grounded–the centeredness, or self-centeredness: the condition of being centered within the self. It resides below the surface of the physical self, which was discussed in chapter one, and resonates deep within the physical being where we are able to tap into our ethereal being to create structure in our life. It can be compared to the soil where the seeds of creation take root, a nourishing soil that must be rich and abundant. And our Foundation must be like the roots of the Oak tree that establish a strong hold in the earth allowing the tree to grow and maintain an unwavering and secure foothold in the ground where it has been planted. Regardless of how powerful the winds of change blow, the tree may bend, but rarely break. This is the strength and structure that needs to be established within the self so that our lives may endure the many trials we face and before we can begin the process of Creation, which I will discuss in chapter five.

There exist various levels of the human form in its Earthly incarnation. First, there is the physical body itself, which was discussed in chapter one. As we move beyond the physical body, we begin to sense the mental composition of the self, as discussed in chapter three, the conscious and subconscious where thoughts are created. And in this next phase, we acknowledge the emotional being as another facet of the human form. We are human beings in physical form radiating electromagnetic thoughts experiencing the full potential of our selves via the dimension of feelings.

As part of the astrological wheel, this is the lowest section of one's astrological chart; it is the midnight point, the deepest part of the astrological composition. This is where the nurturing of all things during the Earthly existence are cultivated and take hold. This section has its association with the Moon and Cancer, the zodiac sign it rules.

The Moon represents the Mother principal, which, in our lives, is where the nurturing process begins. Are we not nurtured within the womb for nine months in the physical body of our Earthly mother? Metaphysically, we have close connections to the physical home, as well, the place where we choose to nest as physical beings. Do we not, at the end of the day, return to that sacred place in order to revitalize and recharge, nourish and relax physically and, at the higher level of existence, spiritually? The home is of great importance in establishing the Foundations in our lives, for if we do not have an environment in our home that radiates peace and balance, discord and imbalance will emanate to all the areas of our lives once we walk out the door.

Our Earthly homes are significant in that they allow us to establish a strong Foundation so we have the continuing fortitude outside our homes to stand our ground. Just as the physical structure of the home requires a foundation of strength to stand on its own, so, too, is that strength required within our Earthly being enabling us each to stand strong during the course of our lives. I will take this one step further and suggest that this sense of stability, even before it can thrive in the home, must first be established within the self. For is not our body the home which houses the spirit while in its Earthly experience? The Earthly body is the physical home, the temple, the sacred space to house the soul.

Just as the Moon creates the essence of nurturing,

which cultivates the Foundation, the sign Cancer desires the security that is a result of the Foundation that was cultivated from the nurturing.

The Moon, as she effortlessly moves through the changing cycles during her 28-day journey, demonstrates to humanity the innate ebb and flow of the graceful passing of age and time. Once we have established a strong and stable foothold in this Earthly world, this ebb and flow will naturally come to pass when we have the confidence and security in the self.

SELF-CENTEREDNESS

Everything in the Universe is cyclical–spirals spinning, center force, center strong–as we are also when we are centered within our self and grounded onto the earth. Just as the tree looks to the Earth for its nourishment and foundation, so, too, can we humans look to the Earth to remain grounded and nourished. Everything we need to survive in this physical form can come from the Earth, our foundation. An atom is just like a planetary system, and the atom is part of our physical composition; the electrons spiral the nucleus just as the planets revolve around the Sun. The Sun is the center, strength, and life force of all beings on Earth. And just as the Sun provided the building blocks for the creation of the planets, in a metaphysical sense, the Sun is also the foundation of the solar system; however, in this instance we are dealing with the Moon.

The Moon reflects the light of the Sun, illuminating

the Foundation of the Spirit. (We will discuss the spirit of the Sun in the following chapter as we elaborate upon the creativity of the expression of the self that comes from the Sun.) Here, in this instance, is where the Moon will shine, nourishing the Foundation upon which the Spirit shall build its creation. The Moon brings light to where it may be dark, for she lights the shadows of the darkest part of the night and reveals to us where there could be a weakness. Illuminating that weakness allows us the opportunity to transform it into a strength, further enhancing the Foundation.

This energy is within us; it's known as the solar plexus. The solar plexus provides grounding and is the center-strength of our being. In my opinion, the solar plexus is an integral part of Foundations, as well as Creativity, which I discuss in the next chapter. Because it's the physical anchor point among the chakras, the solar plexus helps keep us grounded, thus its association with Foundations. The solar plexus, however, also draws its energy from the Sun, thus its association with the formation of Creativity, our ability to create. When we allow the Moon to shine in the dark of night, illuminating the Spirit, the Sun will rise and bring to humanity the opportunity of creation to a new day!

The solar plexus is a power point in the body, its center located above the navel and below the heart in the midsection of the body. This energy center is the grounding point of the physical body. This is where the etheric umbilical cord of light connects itself to the energy source of the Universe. Its energy spins and radiates, pulsating vibrantly, allowing us to feel safe and secure, centered and grounded. This is where we find the confidence to build and create anything in our lives. The vigor of the established Foundations in our lives will transfer into a strong sense of confidence, but not arrogance. Arrogance, in fact, often masks a lack of self-confidence, and takes form when one chooses to bear false witness; the ego is usually the cause in such matters. (This will be discussed in a later chapter.)

The solar plexus and Foundations, the fourth dimension of human potential, share an association with the essence of emotional centeredness, as well, since there are connections to the Moon in this chapter's human potential aspect. When we feel strong and secure on an emotional level, do we not feel like we can climb the highest mountain and soar like the eagle? Fears, anxieties, inhibitions, they're wiped away. A calmness takes over, a peaceful stillness that is not to be confused with a state of being devoid of emotion, which is a quality that demonstrates a lacking, and will only weaken rather than strengthen the Foundation.

If we are using the model of the atom to represent the concept of Foundation, let us delve just a bit deeper. When we go inside that atom, what do we find as the driving force of this subatomic structure? Nothing. The energy source of this most basic of structures seems to be nothing, but there must be some battery that gives it energy. There is: Spirit.

This is not unlike the solar system. What is driving the movement of the planets? Yes, the gravitational pull of the Sun; but what fuels the Sun? We can divide and subdivide and subdivide yet again until we come to what may seem to be simply nothing, but what you've now learned to be Spirit. Essentially, this is the same principle behind the energy source in the self as it relates to the energy source of this aspect of human potential we refer to as the Foundation dimension.

THE STRENGTH IN SELF-CONFIDENCE

We may view foundation as the energy center of the etheric composition of the Spirit, deeply embedded within the microcosm of the ethereal. This is where intuitive knowingness resides, which I will discuss in chapter twelve where I also mention the etheric Book of Records that delves further into this topic. This is where the "gut" feeling originates and takes hold, forms its basis, establishes a Foundation. Whether or not we choose to elaborate on that feeling is entirely up to the individual Spirit.

The Foundation, in this instance, is energy: the source upon which we draw to build anything we choose to experience. This quality can begin to form and take shape at any point in our lives, although early learning experiences certainly establish themselves in the mind and can effect how a sense of confidence may be programmed. Some may have been born, encoded, with a strong sense of self-confidence (Foundation), which will be evident in the planetary configurations of their birth chart; but for every individual, it is something omnipresent. There are those who will learn to develop inner strength along with a dedicated quality of self-confidence; yet some will experience their evolutionary growth without ever really having a strong Foundation, and through that specific experience they are brought to a higher level on the evolutionary scale.

The strength of the Foundation core that resides in our lives is a characteristic within the self that is not a tangible trait. This trait can more accurately be described as a feeling or sensation, something we, at times, may not have the ability to explain in human words, such as emotions.

The strength and security of the Foundation in our lives is what all else is built upon. As we grow and add our experiences to this essence, we move forward, evolve, in how we create our existence, all the while our inner strength providing our security. People who never develop a sense of security and self-confidence have a weak Foundation, for, in some aspects, Foundation and self-confidence are really one and the same.

Self-confidence will support the Foundation; likewise, the lack of self-confidence can deteriorate the Foundation. Some have an innate sense of self-confidence, and for some it is a latent characteristic of our dimensional selves that is developed later.

NURTURER

In order for anything to grow, care, tenderness, and warmth must be provided. This quality may emerge from the nurturing figures in one's life. This could be exhibited in the traditional mother figure or even the father, depending on the dynamics of the family relationships. It's not something that has to be assigned to a gender-specific parent. It can also come from only one parent or no parent. In order for the foundation essence to have strong roots, it must be nurtured and cultivated so that it will stand the test of time. The manner in which we nurture has been instilled in us by the manner in which we have been nurtured.

If Thought, the creation of which was discussed in chapter three, is to have an opportunity to grow, it must be nurtured and cultivated so that its roots can hold tightly onto the fabric of the etheric being. Once this process unfolds, encoding of the thought is imprinted upon the canvas of the self. Thought can now manifest in physical form.

When a thought has not been nurtured, but rather sabotaged by the negativity of an individual–including the negativity of those in that individual's sphere of influence–that thought has not had the chance to grow. Consider when we plant the seeds of a beautiful spring flower. Unless we give it water and light and warmth (just like human beings need in their physical form), that seed may slowly grow roots; but, with lack of nurturing, it will not have a fighting chance. So, too, is the process of growth for thoughts and ideas.

EMOTIONS

This is the aspect of the human potential where, at times, we may feel the most vulnerable. That vulnerability of this quality of the self may emanate from an instability or weakness in the Foundation of the spiritual self–that cosmic, ethereal energy epicenter that goes beyond what we see as physical while occupying the human form. This quality of the human existence is multifaceted, complex and, at times, a quandary to the self, perhaps because emotions are so intangible that we in our humanness seek something concrete we can grab and hold onto and see with our physical eyes. We do not "see" love; we see the physical manifestation of our actions and reactions to the internal sensations as experienced by the Spirit.

Anger, frustration, sadness, and joy are simultaneously individual emotions and aspects of the emotional self. These traits are what give the essence of the Foundation strength, stamina, and durability. One who is seen as "weak" in emotion may not demonstrate the capabilities needed to carry out a task that may require a resolute disposition.

OUR SACRED SPACE: OUR HOMES

The place where we spend that quiet time, the time when we can go within, recharge and regroup, the place that is our sanctuary, the space we go to when we need to escape the mundane and bathe ourselves in solace and sanctity: this is our home, our sacred space. This is the physical essence of the Foundation in our lives. Earlier, I referred to the etheric essence. From there we have emerged to the physical, in this case, the home where the physical body inhabits.

Peace, harmony, and tranquility must reside in this place if we are to recognize and respect those virtues outside the physical home. As the Moon herself represents the peaceful and graceful ebb and flow of life, so, too, must this peaceful flow radiate within the physical home; the ease of this life flow must be at hand in the physical home. When we exist in accordance with the progression of the seasons of life, are we not synchronized with its ebb and flow? As nature changes with the seasons and the trees surrender their leaves baring their limbs and branches to face the harshness of the winter, so do we, as humans, learn to adapt to the ever-changing tides of life in the Foundation of our homes.

Once we have established the strength of foundation within the essence of our being, there is greater ease with that progression of life, for we do not fear that the rising tides or the winds of change will shatter the home. We know we have built steadfast and true a Foundation that is solid and unwavering. This quality will radiate from within the self to the external home, so touted the prophet Kahlil Gibran who stated that the home is the larger body, the extension of the physical and spiritual self.

When we cross the threshold into the home of one who possesses a high spiritual vibration and is steadfastly centered within the self, do we not sense the essence of that radiance? Within that home, there is an atmosphere of peacefulness and tranquility. The adornments of that home may not necessarily be gold fixtures and marble floors, for these are simply external, material objects. The home may be unadorned or decorated only with the simplest of things, yet a sense of magnificence will radiate because it is a reflection of the one who dwells within that place, not the ornamentation.

I have traveled across many oceans during the seasons of my life. In each journey I have learned, in accordance with the Foundation within myself, that wherever I go, I bring my "home" with me. I have remembered that part of my self that allows me to go with the ebb and flow of life, and I bring with me the strength of my Foundation to create that peace (and piece) of my home wherever I am, whether it is among the Alps of Austria or the deserts of Dubai.

We may experience the polar opposite of what I just explained when we enter the home of one who does not demonstrate the essence of centeredness, but rather chaos and commotion. For example, a scattered mind might manifest itself as exorbitant amounts of clutter and mess in the home. This is likely a direct reflection of the state of the mind of the home's occupant(s). One who may be considered a pack-rat has the inability to let go of his past and baggage, therefore physically creating the reality of that condition of the mind within the home. This quality may also manifest because one refuses to move forward with the personal progression of his life. Let me state that I, too, can be guilty of this shortcoming; for many months my home office was in a state of disarray. Once I understood that it was my own hesitance to accept success, I was able to not only clean up my home office, but more readily manifest my own success and move forward.

When we see the home as a place of sanctity and reverence, we gain a different sense of respect for that environment than if it were just a place to hang our hats–or in my case, hang my cape. The physical home is a larger extension of the physical body. Once we have escalated to a sense of awareness, which will be discussed in chapter eleven, we will realize that our planet Earth is a macrocosmic home of the physical body, as well.

SPIRITUAL SECURITY

The spiritual security aspect of the Foundation potential relates to the physical human in its state of being as it experiences the relationship with itself (its Spirit) during its Earthly experience. In addition to its interaction with itself, the human being exists in co-relationship with the etheric dimension as it progresses on the plane of evolution, accordingly co-creating reality with the All That Is. This is the omnipresent connection (spiritual security) with divinity that allows the human being to remain in a state of "groundedness" while it experiences the human existence. And this is the Foundation created beyond the physical and etheric, the essence of the self that is connected to the Foundation of the Universe and the All That Is.

We begin to understand the self in terms of its sense of spirituality and how that sense of who we are on the spiritual plane gives power to the foundation so that we may emerge outside the self and progress to other aspects of this human potential, weaving this thread into all Earthly experiences. In this instance when we refer to spirituality, we are not associating it with what is considered organized religion, which will be elaborated upon in chapter nine, but rather with the transcendent, divine self.

Spiritual security takes root as an aspect of the essence of Foundation as we experience this life's journey and we begin to define who it is we are and what it is we are striving to become. In other words, this is the beginning of Faith–which will culminate as the Knowing discussed in chapter twelve.

This spiritual security is our connection to the Universe, which is our nourishment and "groundedness" that allows the strength of our Foundations to take hold. The sense of what is known as spiritual must radiate from deep within the self and then manifest in the physical world.

FOUNDATIONS, SOLID AND SECURE

And now we understand the significance for the creation of a Foundation, one that is unshakeable, imperishable and unyielding in our everyday existence, so that everything we choose to create may stand on solid footing. The nurturing that transcends into the Foundation radiates from the Moon, which is a reflection of the Sun's light coming to Earth, casting light where there may be darkness, light that in the day will warm and nurture the Earth and at night, when it may seem dark, will shed light and understanding. The nurturing manifests this security into something we can relate to. The sign Cancer desires security, the security that radiates from the nurturing of a stalwart and stable Foundation.

However well built and indestructible the Foundation, during the course of life it may require modification and alteration to suit the needs of the self. This is the innate to the ebb and flow of life's progression. We must learn to adapt to these changes and go with the flow if we are to move forward with the continuation of our existence. Just as a family that has outgrown a home may require modifications to the original structure or even an additional foundation upon which to extend the home with new structure, as we progress through the stages of life, we may find the need to further reinforce or restructure the personal Foundation according to the needs of the self. And this entails the spiritual security of the self. This sense of spirituality is something progressive as defined both for and by the self according to the experiences of the individual. This spiritual Foundation of the umbilical cord of light, which connects us to the centeredness of the Universe, brings nourishment to the physical and etheric self while the spirit occupies this human form.

five
Creativity

*Cherish your visions and your dreams
as they are the children of your soul, the
blueprints of your ultimate achievements.*
—NAPOLEON HILL

Now that we have established a Foundation that is steadfast, unyielding and invincible, we can begin building upon that groundwork by establishing those realities we would choose to experience during our Earthly visit by accessing our Creativity.

We have come to this Earthly understanding as creative beings, and through our Creativity we demonstrate the potential of our planetary arrangement at birth–our astrological composition, human potential–either congruous with our desires or in a manner that is not expressive of the true essence of our being. As I have always emphasized, the choice is ours as to how any occurrence in our life can and will be demonstrated. When we make choices and decisions with awareness and in agreement with our souls' desires, we have the opportunity to create the reality we truly aspire to experience.

The energies for Creativity, our creative abilities, the experience of Love, as well as our children–for are they not a form of creative expression?–emanate from the nearest star, our Sun, which feeds the Earth with energy and warmth. And it's no coincidence that Leo also has associations with these qualities as it is the sign of the zodiac ruled by the Sun. The fire of the Sun and the dramatic qualities of Leo fuel the creative forces, which, at times, can become a theatrical combustion of fire and flame. And astrologically, the heart and one's Soul is represented by the Sun, for as the heart vibrates and pulsates, so does the Sun in the center of our solar system. The heart is the place with which we associate the sensation of Love radiating from the body.

The solar (Sun) plexus proves to have a kind of dual connotation in this instance, just as it did with Foundations. If you'll remember from chapter four, I discussed how the solar plexus acts as an anchor to the structure of the Foundation potential in the human condition. In this instance, it assists in fueling the fires of Creativity that can be built upon that Foundation. Just as the Sun is the center of our solar system, in a way creating a "grounding" quality for all the planets and providing a structural foundation for our planetary system, the Sun is also the energy source, the creative source, of the heavenly bodies. Without the centeredness and grounding of the Sun's gravity, the planets would simply go careening around the Universe, crashing and colliding with each another like billiard balls.

CREATIVITY WITH AWARENESS

On the metaphysical level, Creativity is a dynamic energy that encompasses all individuals. It is the fire of desire and the need for personal expression. However, we may not always be aware of our Creativity or precisely how we express that dynamic quality. Once we have tapped into the creative potential within ourselves, we step up to the next level: using those energies and abilities to create. Then, finally, we reach the level of creation with awareness–this is the higher octave of Creativity, which will be covered in chapter eleven.

Artistry is an obvious example of how Creativity comes to fruition through the craftperson's personal medium. From the way Creativity is inspired, such as the songwriter who is touched by a muse in the still of the night, to the way it is expressed, such as the actor who dramatizes a role on stage or in film, so, too, this form of expression manifests within and out of every individual human being.

We agree artistic talent is creative, but what about the ones who choose to remain in the home and raise their children? Are they not creative? What about a janitor or mechanic or the toll collector on the highway? These individuals are creative beings, as well, although in our sometimes flawed humanness, we may not perceive them to be so, for their Creativity may not be as blatant as that of a concert pianist or impressionist painter. We often discount the potential of those who are outside the artistic/theatrical realm to be creative; however, in every fiber of our being we have the creative potential that can be expressed at any moment as we so choose. This is our nature, to be meaningful through our Creativity.

SOMETHING FROM NOTHING

Creativity is expressive, enriching, invigorating. Have you ever pleasantly surprised yourself after creating something marvelous from what was absolutely nothing only moments before, from transforming nonexistence into existence? For example, a chef will choose the simplest of ingredients, combine them, then, in a manner unique to his creative energy, transform those simple things into something complex, a visual masterpiece and a feast for all senses. Or examine the ingenuity of the gifted mechanic who instinctively knows how to improve the performance of an engine just by making simple adjustments or even knows how to build a better engine. Or better yet, look at Albert Einstein, who conceived the Theory of Relativity; this was truly created from nothingness, for he didn't have tangible items like the chef or the mechanic to complete his project, yet he gained worldwide prominence for his accomplishment.

You can argue that Einstein didn't create from nothing because he used paper and pencil, but those were only tools to bring his concept into reality like the mechanic's wrench or the chef's pots and pans. The finished product for the chef's dinner or the mechanic's engine don't include the pots, pans or wrenches; and the Theory of Relativity can be presented in any form–paper and pencil, printed book, computer screen–but the theory remains the same.

During my high school and university days–which now seem like another life–I would spend many, many hours in the basement of my home sitting at my potter's wheel taking lumps of clay and spinning them into some exquisite form. Many people would tell me how amazed they were by my ability to take a lump of earth and some water and, quite literally, breathe life into the form, creating something of beauty. Those around me would marvel at the transformation, which ultimately filled me with satisfaction for my creative expression. Creativity allows us the vehicle for the expression of the self, as well as providing the opportunity of personal growth.

LOVE, ACTUALLY.

The experience of Love can be one of the highest forms of Creativity we may encounter while existing in human form on this Earth plane. Someone once taught me that true love–whatever that may be–is the only part of ourselves that is not human; it is Divine. When we experience Love, the essence of who we are transcends human boundaries. When we experience the state of being "in love," do we not feel that we can conquer any battle and scale the most challenging of mountains? I suppose that's where the saying "Love conquers all" comes from.

Through the sensation of love–and this does not pertain only to romantic experiences we encounter with another–we often feel as though we are elevated to a euphoric point that seems outside our physical selves. This joyful sensation when experienced with crystal clarity can push one to express Creativity beyond what may exist in our imagination. This is Creativity in its purest form. When Creativity is thwarted, a person's energy becomes stifled. His thirst for that euphoric feeling remains unquenched because he does not have the opportunity to express himself Creatively; consequently, he will often turn to the abuse of substances in an effort to unsystematically reach that plateau. It has been my observation that when Creativity is muted, the individual turns to drugs and alcohol or even food, for when food is consumed gluttonously, it also becomes a form of substance abuse.

In the act of conveying Love for another, we experience a part of ourselves that we are not aware of until it is expressed in relationship with another individual.

However, if we are to experience a shared Love that is absolute, we must first experience clarity of Love for the self. If we enter into an experience with another in hope of finding a love within the self, or to compensate for a lack in another part of our life, we may very well thwart any opportunity to experience through the interaction with another that which we cannot experience alone. A true Love experience will bring opportunity, not obligation to or from another. The opportunity is the Creativity we express in and with the dynamics of another.

Untainted Love will allow the creative experience to unfold without boundaries once it is allowed to progress without expectations, but rather with anticipation of the opportunity of what may transpire through the experience and expression of Love with another.

THE LOVE IN THE MIRROR

What we see in another is the manifestation of a part of our selves–be it physical or beyond what is physical–for we are mirrors of each other. There are moments when we may act without awareness, or perhaps the case may be that past issues, which we may not have resolved, appear in whom we call our beloved. In the reflection, we see a deep-seated wound that needs tending. The Love we've created/attracted may have been done so to bring our own issues to the foreground in order to present ourselves with the opportunity to resolve those issues. Prior to the manifestation of this Love experience, there may have festered within the individual inklings of past memories that influence the fruition of the Love experience. It's our unconscious way of creating the opportunity to rectify our foibles.

Nothing can come to pass in the Universe unless, on some level, both parties involved are in agreement. Somewhere along the atmospheric continuum, lover and beloved agreed that there would be a union, so that both can experience from one another something that resonates within them. And through the manifestation of their union, the expression of this occurrence will come into form.

RELATIONSHIPS IN FORM

Many unconsciously recreate in their own relationships with a beloved the way one or both parents expressed themselves in their relationship(s). This learned relationship behavior can also find its way into a workplace relationship, as well, but for the purpose of this section's discussion, we will review how that may come to pass in a love relationship.

Unless we are willing to take a risk–another aspect of Creativity on deck for discussion later in this chapter–by reviewing the dynamics of our behavior in our interaction with a beloved, we cannot fully become aware of past influences in love affairs. If the relationship between individuals is one of positive and pure expression, the desire to understand its machinations may not be urgent or persistent. However, if we consistently create a relationship that is less than loving (as simple as argumentative or as great as oppressive and abusive) and yet perceive it to be an expression of Love, then we must examine past influences to confront the cause and, consequently, effect a change for the better.

Let me illustrate an example of how a lover relationship has negative potential. A love relationship that demonstrates itself with violence–domestic or otherwise–anger, and abuse to the individual is what he equates Love to be and how he perceives he must experience it. Bear in mind that this is something that is not always created on the conscious level. Obviously, people do not usually go out into the world professing a wish to experience a love relationship in which they will be on the receiving end of a baseball bat. This encoding is something very deep within the psyche of the individual. There may not be a conscious memory of this reality until it is brought to form (i.e., the negative relationship is actualized). However, I will state that something must exist somewhere inside one's self in order for this to come to pass.

I'm certain this concept may not be well received by most; but, I know, without doubt, that all that comes to pass in the Universe must be in accordance with the will of the Universe. We simply may not be consciously aware of how those vibrations within our being brought us to the experience. I will also state that we may apply this truth to any experience that comes to pass in this existence and the next. At one point in my life, I found myself experiencing a verbally and physically abusive relationship. Though the relationship didn't last long, it was not until several years had passed that I achieved clarity and awareness about how this "love" experience was created through my unconscious thoughts of what I equated love to be.

A media outlet once interviewed me immediately following the passing of Johnny Cochrain. I was asked what I believe to have transpired once Johnny met Nicole Simpson and Ron Goldman on "the other side." It is my understanding that they came together in some cosmic coffee house, if you will, to provide them with the opportunity to discuss (now, with clarity and awareness) why they chose the experience they did (at the etheric level, of course) and how, through that experience, their individual souls have progressed along the evolutionary scale. Their Earthly beings may not have consciously stated, "I want to be part of a murder/love/mystery high-profile homicide case," but their agreement was sealed on the etheric level.

CREATING PURE LOVE

When two individuals come together with no expectation, obligation, or need for self-validation, the doors to the experience of a union filled with pure Love and joy are opened further than what we can comprehend. Alas, for this to come to pass, we must proceed with openness to the "knowing" of that possibility. Many clients have come to me over the years and asked, "Where is it that I can begin to look for Love?" I would reply that we must not "look" for Love, for if we are in the process of looking for Love, all we will do is look for Love, thus leaving no opportunity to receive it. In order for the true expression of that experience we define as Love to enter our life, we must allow, and not *look* for, Love to come to us. Our minds and hearts must be permitted to become open to the experience we desire; once we allow ourselves to come to that point, we can begin the creative process of conceiving a union filled with the Love and joy we desire.

When we come together as lover and beloved and we are brought to a place that we can arrive at only when we are in communion with that certain individual, we begin to experience the purest form of creation and joy in the expression of that Love. We must know in our hearts and minds that Love will manifest in our lives; and only then can we experience the fruition of Love in form.

Another Side of Love

The sensation that I have been describing as Love does not necessarily have to take the form of two individuals exchanging their dynamic energy. We have the ability to experience this sense of euphoria when we express, Creatively, something that reflects our true essence.

Let me provide an example from my own existence.

My Love affair, my joy, my sense of creative expression and fulfillment, comes in the joyful experience of my knowledge of astrology and sharing that part of myself with others, as well as the creative process of my writing. Through this experience, observing and understanding the potential of the planetary compositions and the influence of their energies in co-creation with humanity, comes my life's joy–pure and simple. And my ability to convey this information through the writing I create also brings to me a sense of love. I choose to direct these energies into something positive, fulfilling, and humanitarian, hence creating in my life the joy and satisfaction of a loving experience.

Love need not take its form in the interaction of two individuals; it may find its expression through a creative action that demonstrates an aspect of the individual's human potential. When we have the experience of demonstrating our true potential, we find ourselves experiencing the sensation of "being in Love."

CHILDREN

The experience of the conception and the birth process of a child is one of the most natural forms of creative expression for humans, as well as other members of the animal kingdom. I feel this is nature's purest, most powerful, means of creative expression possessed by humans in the experience of "being." We have the innate ability to create life just as was done by the creative power of the Divinity of the Universe. This is another example of the All That Is dwelling within each and every living organism on the planet and in the Universe.

As the power of creation breathed life into the fabric of our humanness, so, too, do we create life in the same manner. As the Greatness created the Heavens and the Earth, so, too, do we create our realities; we have that same power within our being. In this instance–the conception of children–we create extensions of ourselves made up of the same DNA that is encoded with the electromagnetic pulse of our being.

The child is a creative expression and an extension of the self, as well as the manifestation of the union of two individuals. This little bundle of joy will demonstrate qualities of both parents, as well as its karmic connections, which have been intertwined and impressed into the dynamics of this union over many millennia. Along with the genetic coding of the individual, there is also an impression instilled within the psyche of the child as it observes behaviors of the family into which it has been born. There are, of course, those traits and characteristics that run within the bloodline of a child; however, when behaviors have been repeated over the course of generations, and when the same principles, ideologies, lifestyle patterns have been allowed to repeat themselves, they are also programmed into the child–thus, the "sins" of the father/mother are passed on to the children. When an angry parent yells, "You're just like your father/mother," the parent is affirming that the child is simply repeating the behaviors it has observed.

When conditions and behaviors that do not produce desirable outcomes have been allowed to repeat themselves without awareness of the need for change, generations upon generations pay the price of an unwise choice that may have been made hundreds of years prior.

An easily illustrated example is alcohol or physical abuse. This condition may have manifested and been repeated over many generations and unless the patterns are broken, it will be allowed to continue until the behavior becomes thwarted. In this instance, the creative forces of the child's experience in an alcoholic household produce a situation of negativity, toxicity, and, in some instances, abuse that may have been and may still be repeated for many, many years.

For example, let say a child observes the alcoholic behavior of his father. The father may have also observed alcohol abuse in his house while growing up, and after years of observing this behavior, it became ingrained within him as a normal part of adulthood. As he grows, alcohol becomes a part of his recreational activities with friends, schoolmates, at family functions. Getting drunk is no big deal. "Doesn't everybody do it?" he asks himself. Perhaps his father wasn't an angry or violent drunk. Maybe he just drank until he passed out. And when he becomes a father, he does the same. He drinks until he's drunk. Some may not even view this as alcohol abuse, because he's not really harming anyone, but those people deceive themselves. He is harming someone. Himself, for one. And those impressionable people around him who will pick up this addictive behavior.

I will forego the many possibilities that can occur due to his drunkenness and stick to the vicious cycle. Now his child, say a daughter, grows up observing the same behavior. Unless something or someone changes the child's opinion of the father's drinking behavior, she will continue in her father's footsteps, and her grandfather's footsteps. Something must make that daughter aware of the condition she's in or she will remain in the vicious cycle prolonged by her forefathers. Perhaps a friend, who does not view the behavior as normal, encourages her to seek help to come to terms with the death of her father due to drunk driving or cirrhosis of the liver. Whatever the inciting incident, without some awareness, these conditions will continue and repeat until, at some point in one of the generations of that family, there comes that moment of awareness and the circle is finally broken.

This process of creation is a continuum through the generations, but there are those instances when a child will come into this world who will rise above his or her conditions and create great change and transformation; this, of course, can alter the course of the generations that follow. The child prodigy will certainly stand out among others.

When You See a Chance

The risks we take and the decisions we make are part of our creative process and expression of that Creativity. It may not seem outwardly obvious that taking a risk is something creative, but when we think about the fundamental nature of the process, we do need to have some sort of Creativity in the orchestration of what it is we are going to do so that the end result will be beneficial and fruitful.

For example, can't the conception of a child be seen as a risk? We have no idea how bringing a child into our lives will affect everything we do. Nor can we predict the temperament or physical health of the child, and those two factors can wreak havoc in our perfectly mapped family plan. If we examine the planetary energies of a child at his birth, we are looking at the potential for his life in his chart. However, it is not until that child begins to grow, develop, and demonstrate his free will that we can observe how the child has chosen to manifest those energies. Will he strive to meet his human potential?

Taking risks can be stressful, but it can also create wonderful opportunities. For example, when one makes the decision to resign from a job that may have provided a cushy life in order to devote more time to nurture his dreams, this individual has certainly taken a risk, a gamble if you will, in pursuit of a more fulfilling life. In the process of creating something out of nothing, there is a sense of uncertainty in the outcome.

We may find ourselves moving along with the process of creation, formulating concepts and ideas, fabricating and formulating our thoughts into something that may not take physical form. The risk of this creation is that we really do not know what the outcome will be. We can speculate and hypothesize; however, the true "knowing" of the outcome will not be realized until the situation has come to pass. This is the risk involved in Creativity–we just do not know what the result of our Creativity will be.

When we fall in love, are we not taking a risk? When we bring children into this world, we are taking a risk, as well. These are all part of the creative process I have been discussing in this part of our journey.

When we dedicate ourselves to a methodical thought process of Creativity in taking a risk, the end result will be as beneficial as the process itself. When one chooses to resign from a long-term corporate position to embark upon the pursuit of a dream, she is taking a risk; however, the result can be positive if she devotes time to positive thought and planning of the process for this dream-chase. Herein lies the Creativity of the risk-taking. There needs to be a sense of Creativity in the ideas, the creation of a game plan–similar to that of a football team's playbook–for the individual to follow. When the dream-chase is followed through in a methodical manner, the risk can be beneficial, provided all else is allowed to fall into place and the risk-taker doesn't trip herself up in some self-defeating manner.

The condition of excessive gambling can be seen as a creative experience. However, the energies that have been directed into that particular form of expression are not necessarily beneficial to the existence of the individual. This is an example of a being filled with Creativity who implements no true creative expression of the self except in the emotional experience of the risk. I do not mean to trivialize this condition, which, in excess, is a disease. I simply state that this behavior, when in excess, can be a result of one's frustration with his lack of creative expression.

CREATING LIFE, CREATIVE LIVING

And so we, in this physical manifestation of humanness, have come to this experience as creative beings, encoded with the all-encompassing creative force of the Universe. In the Bible, the first book of Genesis is all about the creative force of the Universe and the All That Is.

The center of our planetary system, our Sun, can be viewed as the creative energy of our solar system and the planets are its children born out of the cosmic chaos that was channeled into creation, symmetry, and perfection. It radiates and pulsates as the heart of the physical body it represents, and the blood that is pumped through the body can be seen as the creative juices of the energy flow of the Universe. The Sun's counterpart, Leo, shares these qualities as we move along the astrological path.

The essence of Creativity in each and every one of us can manifest itself in the form of the expression of Love. The experience of Love can be made known with another individual or through a means of creative expression. When we move to a place where we are choosing the experience of Love, not out of a need for something that may be lacking in the individual, but for the opportunity of that which we cannot experience without the inclusion of another human being, we open the door to opportunity and not codependency. And when we seek salvation in the experience of a relationship with another, that relationship may last for a while, but the quality of the experience will be lessened and we will always be in "need" of the other, creating a codependent experience.

Creativity affords us the opportunity for personal expression that can demonstrate itself in the birth of our children, in the experience and expression of love, and with the creation of risk. In that process, though we are uncertain of the outcome of our creativity in the process of formulating the risk, we become creative, regardless.

six

Health and Well-being

*The doctor of the future will give no
medicine, but will interest her or his
patients in the care of the human frame,
in a proper diet, and in the cause and
prevention of disease.*
–THOMAS A. EDISON

I f we are to choose to live a life in which we manifest
our human potential to its fullest, we must experience the condition of existing in a body that operates at optimum capacity. Anything less and we're just
functioning at half wattage. The human body has been
divinely designed so that it creates a balance when there
is imbalance–just as nature does–when we allow it to do
so. It has the power and potential to heal itself, when it
is allowed to function as it was designed: without external interference, i.e. the various assortment of synthetic
drugs we choose to ingest such as aspirin or antibiotics.

The sign of the zodiac that rules Health and Well-being is Virgo. Its planetary ruler, Mercury, presides over this aspect of the human potential, as well. As we discussed in chapter three, the planet named for the Messenger of the Gods governs the mind and the mental process, so it would hold true that the condition of the mind strongly influences the condition of the body. Even the medical profession has acknowledged that one's attitude (in other words, the condition of the mind) and desire to heal the self does, in fact, aid in the healing process of the body. The interference of foreign matter, such as antibiotics, in the body only delays and interrupts the body's natural ability to heal, which, in fact, will also delay and hinder the body's natural ability to equalize any imbalance.

We, in our somewhat primitive humanness, feel we must meddle with this process of natural healing because, of course, we know better. We *are* human, after all. We feel we must intervene with matter foreign to the body, i.e. medications and the various forms of designer drugs, which impede the natural process of the body's innate ability to heal itself. Let me *strongly* state at this point, as I am certain this material will be taken out of context, that I am not advocating that everyone abandon any medical regimen, thwart any efforts made by their personal physicians, and simply throw logic out the window. I am simply offering an alternative perspective to something that may not be effective or in accordance with our body's natural abilities.

I do suggest a Health-maintenance program designed for the individuality of each human form. As much as we are all alike, our individuality defines how our bodies respond to outside stimuli–food, exercise, vitamins and any other source that may affect the performance of the body–and we should approach Health maintenance in an appropriate manner. This can be through a process of elimination, as what may be successful for one may not necessarily have the same result for another. There is also learning to sense, to "know," exactly what the body needs, and this ability is something that can be developed over time when we permit ourselves to be in tune with our body's requirements.

FINDING YOUR WAY THROUGH THE DARK

How we exist in the form of the body can directly or indirectly affect how and to what extent we manifest the full potential of the human experience. The breathing in and the breathing out symbolize a rhythm–it is the rhythm of the Universe. We may ponder the question: "Am I functioning in accordance with the pulse of the Universe and striving for an optimum physical existence by the manner in which I am living my everyday life or am I just existing and meandering through each day?"

Most individuals are not living a balanced existence–most may not be aware of the damage done to the body through the ingestion of matter that nature did not intend for the human body to consume. To understand the divinely designed intent of a substance, we can examine its place and purpose in nature. Again, these offerings come from what I have experienced through my existence and during my personal process of realizing my human potential.

For example, milk is not intended for human consumption, but rather for the mother cow to feed its calf. Beyond our years of feeding from our mother's breast, milk is not something pertinent to our existence, although the dairy industry would have us believe differently. The human body lacks the proper enzyme needed for the complete digestion of the milk substance, which is why many individuals, without knowing, are lactose intolerant. I would suggest performing a trial of elimination in which you remove dairy products from your diet and then take notice how the body reacts. You may be surprised how much greater the efficiency of the digestion process will become. Again, this is not the end-all to proper nutrition, just a suggestion.

Substances such as drugs, alcohol, and cigarettes create toxicity in the body that can result in an imbalance of the body's functions. I am actually astounded that in this day and age we still choose to subject our bodies to toxicity regardless of all the information available about the proven dangers of such practices. Metaphysically, when one chooses to partake in behavior such as the consumption of drugs and alcohol, the etheric body forms an attraction to "low-level negative entities."

These can be fallen angels, dark spirits, even what some may call demons, but most simply, a negative energy being. Let me provide a metaphor, and once again, this is *my* deduction as a result of *my* Earthly experience. I simply offer a point to ponder.

Most social places where alcohol and cigarettes, as well as other designer drugs, are consumed are usually concentrated to bars and nightclubs. (I should point out that most U.S. states now prohibit smoking in public establishments.) This environment is primarily dark, low lights, loud music–most of which is barely comprehensible–the rooms are filled with toxic, secondhand smoke and, for the most part, it is difficult to really see and hear another person. This is, in part, a dark, low-level vibration of energy concentrated in one location multiplied by each individual. This is not to say one should not partake in the aforesaid activities. Rather, simply review the conditions of the surroundings and evaluate if such activities are conducive to the existence truly desired.

Just as we have come to know there are those dark energies that exist in the spirit dimension, there are cousins to those spirits that exist in human form, as well. Humanity is spirit that exists in physical form, but at the subatomic level, we are no different from those in the spirit world–we are just housed in a physical, human body. Those energies in the spirit world that radiate low-level vibrations are similar to their counterparts in human form who simply lack awareness, and in most instances it's an awareness of light. There is a darkness that surrounds them, so they attract the vibration of other dark energies.

So how does this pertain to my earlier statement about dwelling in those dark places? When any consumption, even the smallest amount, of alcohol, drugs or any matter that alters the mind and body, has been ingested, the mind moves to a distorted state. This is Psychology 101. The perceptions become impaired, the brainwaves of the mind begin to slow down, and the body's response time is lessened.

When the brain slows to a low-level brainwave frequency in an unnatural fashion, it is exposed to that which is buried deep in the mind. These may be past, subconscious memories, some which may be difficult to confront, especially when the mind in its awakened state is not prepared to do so. In this state of being, one may experience behavior that may not be characteristic of the individual, or one may undergo the experience of being a "happy drunk." Regardless, when the vibration of the spirit is lowered in a manner that is not self-controlled because the mind has been exposed to an altered state of consciousness unnatural to the mind/body connection, the spirit of the being becomes susceptible to any passing negative vibration, spirit, entity, etc.

This is also characteristic of one placed under anesthesia. When individuals emerge from that altered state, many find themselves awakened in tears without any logical explanation why these emotions were experienced. It is my understanding that while in that altered state, the brain frequency is unnaturally lowered to the slow vibration of the theta brainwave frequency. Deep in these regions are where painful memories are stored, the recollection of traumatic experiences reside, and anything that may be too painful for the conscious mind to deal with is suppressed. While in that state of consciousness, the essence of the being is quite literally forced to "see" these situations, so upon awakening, the memory is experienced by the spirit, but not in the awakened conscious of the individual.

These memories dwell in all the rooms of the mansion of the spirit. They may not always be apparent to the spirit, for in the spirit world, as well as in this Earthly kingdom, that which we choose to not see will always be our choice. It matters not if we are in the human form or at the higher vibration of the Spirit dimension; we are always at choice as to how, what, and where we choose to deal with any experience or past memory.

I stated earlier that the spirit dimension exists at a lower brainwave frequency (alpha) and during meditation we can communicate and interact with that dimension. Meditation is a controlled situation, but with the introduction of drugs and alcohol, which alter the mind in a manner over which we really have no control, we are open and susceptible to all that is negative dwelling in the spirit dimension. These energies literally attach themselves to the spirit, leaving the individual to wonder why he has no conscious explanation why his life is in the dire state it is in.

Though we all possess different beliefs or interpretations about the existence of Hell, this place of darkness that I'm talking about is, quite literally, where Hell exists. In other words, **H**eaven **E**xisting at a **L**ow **L**evel. When we are not operating at our full potential, and when we slip away into that part of the human/spirit realm devoid of light, we are experiencing the condition of Hell. We find ourselves operating at a low-level vibration. Conversely, the state of being known as Heaven operates at a high-frequency vibration, such as the highest vibration of light that is a pure, vibrant violet. Once we move to a higher vibration of that violet, it is no longer visible to the human eye, but vividly apparent to the spirit dimension.

Food, Glorious Food!

Optimum existence is a balanced mind and body–I would also include the etheric body within this equation. In this section of our discussion, we are reviewing matters pertaining to achieving and maintaining the ideal performance of the physical body. Probably the main and most important ingredient to the recipe of peak performance is a nutrition program that has been designed according to the requirements of optimum operation specific to an individual.

We really are what we eat. If we were to create a visual of each and every substance ingested into our bodies, we might think twice before we consume some of the foods we eat. We must become conscious of what we ingest into our bodies if we're to become in tune with the body and its functions. The result of this awareness is "knowing" what the body needs to nourish itself and when it is needed.

We may ask ourselves, "Are we eating to live or do we live to eat?" We may view eating to live as a necessity of survival in this Earthly form, and living to eat as a manner in which we may compensate for a lack in other areas of our lives. Food releases endorphins creating a "feel good" sensation in the body. Exercise and the emotion of Love can create a similar sensation.

When we move to a level of existence where we become in tune with our physical bodies, we have the ability to recognize what our bodies are *telling* us in terms of what they need to function in a state of balance. We would be wise to pay attention to the manner in which our bodies react when given a particular food. Many individuals experience food allergies without conscious recognition of the fact.

It wasn't until I eliminated dairy products from my food regimen that I learned that dairy really didn't work for my individual body. I would consume luscious protein shakes, albeit with low-fat milk, and experience stomach cramps and assume that the formula of the protein shake was too difficult for my system to digest. In fact, once I experimented with soy milk as a substitute for regular milk in blending my protein drink, I no longer experienced the difficulties with my digestive process. This conclusion evolved through trial and error and, needless to say, I choose to no longer consume dairy products, although there are those rare moments when I do indulge in ice cream–I am still in the human form and desire those Earthly indulgences...on occasion!

Dis-ease

Disease is the body not experiencing a state of ease and balance–the body is not operating at peak and optimum performance. The illness can result from repeatedly thinking a negative thought or performing a negative behavior or subscribing to an unsuitable paradigm until the body no longer has the strength to naturally fight off the toxins. Lung cancer as a result of years of inhaling cigarette smoke–not in all instances, but in some–is a perfect example. Of course, I am not suggesting that anyone quit smoking. That is one's individual choice to consume carbon monoxide, low forms of radiation, as well as other wonderful toxins. I am not here to interfere with the free will of any living and breathing form; I merely offer suggestions based on what I have come to know and understand.

When the body experiences "serious illness" (in the

spirit realm a cold is no different from cancer), it has been allowed over a long period of time the experience of that which is subversive to the healthy manifestation of the physical body. Living in a state of turbulent mental anguish over long periods of time will not only result in a body that does not operate to its full potential or is resistant to disease, but will also create an imbalanced state of mind directly affecting the condition of the body. When I began this chapter, I wrote that the planet Mercury, ruler of the mind, also directly affects the Health of the body; hence the state of mind affects the condition of the body, ergo the saying "mind over matter."

WEAK MIND, WEAK BODY

When our physical bodies demonstrate a state of weakness, the condition may derive from what some refer to as a weak mind. If we refer back to our chapter regarding Foundations, a weak Foundation may result in the weak condition of mind, then ultimately, a weak body. All concepts in this book are interconnected by one aspect or another.

When we are not in our centeredness, when our Foundations are not strong, we may find ourselves distracted, off-center. This creates an imbalance in the body and, as a result, the body experiences symptoms of the imbalance, such as the sniffles from a cold. Though there is no real cure for the common cold–only the symptoms can be treated in hopes that at some point those symptoms will diminish–we can prevent it through the power of positive thinking. A strong mind will, in fact, become equal to a strong Foundation and physical body. When we refuse to "buy into" an illness, we simply do not create that condition in the body. I will shortly discuss how we become the "victim" of the illness.

Wednesday's Child is Full of Woe

Someone may come to me and say, well, what about a five-year-old child, an innocent to the illusions of this world, who develops terminal leukemia? How is that illness created within him? A truly challenging question, yes, and I will do my best to explain this seemingly unfair condition. Again, we are speaking in terms of metaphysics; none of this I declare as absolute, but rather as my experience as it relates to my human experience.

Before the child had embarked upon his journey into this life, it intended to have the experience of the tragic illness–along with its parent, for nothing can come to pass among several individuals unless all are in agreement in the spirit dimension. This, of course, was chosen by both the parents and the individual prior to their entry into their bodies. The intention of that brave soul who succumbs to the terminal illness is to influence those in his personal sphere of existence, and perhaps even someone across the globe, by using the devastation of that experience. Perhaps those individuals who remain once that soul has departed will make choices of their own that benefit humanity as a whole.

A short life–even five years–is a full life when severe illness or death is experienced at an early age. In our state of humanness, we may not always be aware of the divine contracts that particular individual had orchestrated before entering into human form, for through and with those contracts we have come to know ourselves as creative and we experience the evolution of the spirit. This is not to lessen the sadness, but simply to give an alternative understanding to a situation filled with riddle and wonder.

THE POWERS THAT BE

The manner in which we overcome illness can be equal to how we create success in our lives and overcome a seeming failure, or a hurdle along the path of success. I, for one, refuse to buy into an illness–I simply do not have the time to allow my body to become symptomatic nor to sanction my body to function at any performance level other than its highest. I have too much to do, so I choose to do all that resides in my power and within my knowingness to create a state of being in my body that will allow me to continue an optimum existence. As a result, I am able to experience myself in all my humanness to its full potential. This is my choice, and so this is true for me.

The power of maintaining a positive mindset has always been suggested by most healthcare practitioners as being one of the key factors in the success of over-coming an illness. I would suggest we maintain a positive mindset as a preventative measure so that we need not deal with the disruption of disease in our lives.

When we discover ourselves experiencing an illness, we sometimes find ourselves surrendering to the "woe is me" frame of mind–in a way, this is how the drama queen operates. She (or he) strives for the attention she is given when she is in that less than optimal state. This particular behavior may have been instilled at a young age when the only time the individual received attention from her parents was when she was ill–very often this behavior is unconscious. So, the child, being highly intelligent, noticed that when she craved attention, she needed only to be sick! This behavior characteristic became subconscious to the child as she grew into an adult, and so, without conscious knowing, this individ-ual would experience illness after illness.

After an individual conducts himself in this manner over a lifetime, the traits become regimented and unconscious to the point where it would seem as thought the individual has no control over the condi-tion. But control can be regained if approached with awareness and with the will to change the behavior and acknowledge the actions and reasoning of the self. So, do we choose to be the victim and buy into the drama of the illness or the victor and exist in a condition of the mind and body that allows the body to function at its full potential? In other words, do we suffer or serve? As always, the choice is ours.

The manner in which we are creating or not creating drama equates to one's success or failure. One who radiates confidence and success will not bow down to the condition of an illness. Yes, there are those moments when those of great success can experience themselves as symptomatic; however, they deal with the illness with vigor and strength. They simply choose to overcome the illness as they would any hurdle that they may have encountered on the road to their success.

When one lives each day of his life as if it were a chore to simply breathe and then is presented with a debilitating bodily condition, he will probably stay in bed and pull the covers over his head. This is not to imply that the latter is inferior to the former example, simply that the latter is a polar opposite to the individual who does not buy into the "woe is me" mindset of an illness.

HOLISTIC HEALTH

We, as Westerners, find it easier to take a pill as a quick fix for all that ails us as opposed to allowing the body to perform as it was designed to by healing itself and by practicing natural remedies.

We hastily swallow aspirin when we experience a headache. I use this example because it is one for which many have a point of reference. Before allowing the headache to occur, it may be a wise practice not to behave in such a way that will create the headache, such as succumbing to an overabundance of mental anguish. A helpful suggestion may be to view the experience of a headache as the body's method of altering the awakened consciousness in order to perceive the undetected existence of a condition in the body that is out of balance. Instead of quickly running to the pharmacy or medicine cabinet for a pill that will seemingly alleviate all that ails the body, a practice more natural to a well-balanced state of being would be to meditate. In that moment when we experience that discomfort, if at all possible, it would serve the mind and body well to perhaps remove the self from the present activities that may be contributing to the ailment in order to quiet the mind. If we were to allow ourselves a few moments to enjoy deep, healthy breathing, allowing the mind to become free of the anguish and overabundant activity, literally within a few minutes, we may find that we are no longer experiencing the headache, and perhaps instead, a body that is more at ease and peace.

The option of holistic healthcare versus traditional western medicine is always at our choice; we just need to practice that which will allow us to experience the condition of a body that is operating at its full potential. Some of the many options of holistic healthcare include herbs, various relaxation techniques such as meditation, massage, chiropractic adjustments, and acupuncture.

ACHIEVING WELL-BEING

At this dimension of the human potential, we have reviewed the manner in which the mind, Mercury, has influence over the physical body, giving us the ability to create balance or imbalance in the body. Ultimately, we have the power to heal the body when we choose to practice that part of the human potential.

Virgo rules over our physical condition, Health, and Well-being, which is a result of the state of the mind. And so, the planet of the mind and its condition, Mercury, consequently rules over the Kingdom of Virgo.

In order for the human form to operate at its peak performance and thus provide us with the opportunity to experience all that is available to us while we are in the human condition, we must fuel the body with nourishment and nutrients that will produce an existence conducive to reaching our optimum condition. In terms of nutrition, exercise, and healthcare, it's important to follow the natural route that best meets the individual's specific needs and that will allow the body to exist and operate at its full potential. We, as humans, simply need to make different choices regarding what we ingest and perhaps look at healthcare in proactive, preventative terms instead of waiting until illness overtakes the body leaving one to reside in a condition of dis-ease. As the saying goes, "An ounce of prevention is worth a pound of cure."

Knowing the Inner Self

Now that we have completed the first part of our journey to achieve human potential, we can progress beyond the physical, personal surroundings of the self as individual, the Inner Self; we can strive to create a balance for every aspect of the human potential that has been discussed in this first section.

There exists a yin and yang balance between the Internal and External Self. For every point in section one of this book, there exists its complement or higher octave/vibration in section two. The first discussion in the next section will elaborate upon balance, for we as humans must experience a balance to complement all that exists in nature so that we might be in accordance with the natural ebb and flow of the All That Is. Just as we feel the Sunlight of the day, we also see Sunlight reflected off the Moon during the night; in order for us to know and understand the light of the day, we must also experience and explore the darkness of the night.

Section Two

The External Self

*By a peculiar prerogative, not only is
each individual making daily advances in
the sciences, and may make advances in
morality, but all mankind together are
making a continual progress in
proportion as the universe grows older; so
that the whole human race, during the
course of so many ages, may be
considered as one man, who never ceases
to live and learn.*
—BLAISE PASCAL

*You cannot hope to build a better world
without improving the individuals. To
that end each of us must work for his own
improvement, and at the same time share
a general responsibility for all humanity,
our particular duty being to aid those to
whom we think we can be most useful.*
—MARIE CURIE

seven

Balance

The best and safest thing is to keep a balance in your life, acknowledge the great powers around us and in us. If you can do that, and live that way, you are really a wise man.
—EURIPIDES

As we progress outside of the self, hopefully with the consciousness that has been established within the realm of the self that I covered in chapter one, we strive to experience the counterpart of the self and our human potential in the external world. With all interactions on the Earth and those at a higher spiritual dimension, we strive to create a sense of symmetry and balance within the realm of the physical world but outside of the physical self. The second section of this book is titled the External Self, appropriately so since we are now moving out of the Internal Self and focusing on what is outside our physical selves.

The first dimension discussed in this second section of the book no longer concentrates on the individual self, for we come to the awareness that as we exist independently, we also co-exist in relation to one another, as well as with each and every organism that exists on Earth. The focus now turns toward the human potential aspect that strives to maintain equilibrium in life, which can be experienced in the charisma of our partnerships and the delicate balance that needs to be established in those encounters.

In the astrological realm, the sign of the zodiac that is associated with relationships, partnership, companionship, beauty and balance is Libra; Venus is the planet that is associated with these qualities. The beauty that Venus shines upon the adornments, abundance, and material possessions we discussed in chapter two now carries into our partnerships, romantic or otherwise. In this aspect, we are not restricted to the partnerships of the lover/beloved type, but instead touch upon any relationship where two have come together for a grander experience of the human potential.

We discussed in chapter five the experiences surrounding the love relationships and the opportunities that can be experienced in and through those unions; in this chapter, it becomes clear that opportunity presents itself with any relationship or union we choose to experience. In fact, a relationship is sometimes a prerequisite, a necessary opportunity to experience a part of one-self that cannot be accessed through the experience as a single-self unit. The manifestation of those experiences is something that already dwells within the self. However, what is necessary for that quality to present itself is the interaction with another; only then is that characteristic brought to form. It's already within the self; the experience of the interaction with another will bring it from the unconscious self to the conscious reality.

This section will encompass not only partnerships of a romantic nature, but also partnerships that can be established in a business endeavor; in fact, I will include partnerships in any other sense of the word for this discussion. For example, two friends may come together to work on a project, striving to create and achieve a similar goal. These two individuals, neither involved romantically nor initially intent on embarking upon a business venture, have established a partnership. The same would be true of any two individuals who may come together to create and serve a greater purpose, such as conceiving and running some sort of fundraiser. The principles for romantic partnerships also apply to this type of experience, as well. The sense of Balance and the equilibrium needed to establish those relationships is the dynamic energy presented in this section.

Balance, in this instance, is both a condition and an extension of the natural ebb and flow of life's progression. When we learn to go with the flow, we remember that higher part of the self, the part that innately knows, understands, the significance of creating a natural Balance.

When we encounter someone who might be described as a control freak, we are confronted with a person who does not understand the natural ebb and flow, give and take, the Balance of nature that is natural to the self. This condition is a form of imbalance wherein one feels the need to dominate, even manipulate, any situation because that person believes the conditions of the outcome are always in the hand of someone else. This type of instance is brought on by a fear of loss of the self in one form or another. This is a classic case of imbalance. If that person were to acknowledge and employ a higher understanding of themselves as a spiritual being, he or she would gracefully bow to the innate and natural flow of the spirit within the self.

THE BALANCE WITHIN

In order for there to be health and harmony in any relationship, it is necessary to create a healthy Balance within the individual self. This is something that comes with awareness of the self and a true understanding of the nature of the self. Without a sense of knowing who one is, it may be a difficult and daunting challenge when moving into a partnership with the expectation of "finding oneself" within the realm of that relationship. Many of us seek to complete the self and fulfill our lives through a relationship with a significant other only to discover, over time, that a lack of contentment remains.

This aspect is not confined to romantic involvement. It may also be linked to one who is striving to create a strong business. This person may seek out a business partner who he believes demonstrates the qualities of someone who can help him achieve his goals; however, if the give and take is not equal or balanced, the relationship can go awry.

For example, the individual with the lesser skills may sit back, making no effort to learn from the other, and the individual with the greater business skills may feel resentful that the other is making no effort and cannot, or will not, carry his weight. Conversely, if both individuals are balanced and entering the business relationship with an open mind and open heart, the one lacking the skills will be eager to learn from the other and work hard to prove himself while the one with the greater skills will not resent giving a little extra, secure in the knowledge that his partner will eventually give back when he's able. So, if both come into the experience with this understanding, both parties can benefit. If not, an imbalance will occur that will create struggle and strain within the dynamic of the relationship.

This sense of Balance must reside within the self before it can carry over to any coexistence. The Balance within the self will also create a sense of harmony and peacefulness within the self.

BALANCE IN, BALANCE OUT

An imbalance in a relationship can cause an imbalance within one (or both) of the individuals, especially if the individual came into the experience with a great sense of personal Balance. And this personal Balance can easily become disrupted over time without the individual knowing it. There are those moments when we feel we can influence others if we have that sense of Balance within our selves; however, sadly, if the other individual does not exude that sense of Balance within and does not choose to create that quality within the self, our efforts will be thwarted.

As these two individuals continue along this path of disproportion, the balanced person will undoubtedly lose the sense of Balance that he may have strived to create over a long period of time. This example is apropos of how one of imbalance can negatively influence one of Balance. There is a shift in the electromagnetic energy of the aura fields (the energy field that surrounds every living organism, which we will discuss in a later chapter) of both people: one individual spirit striving to create Balance and the other spirit fighting either to maintain control over the other or to resist change. Either way, the balanced spirit cannot overcome the conflict of imbalanced energy.

When we are moving outside the realm of ourselves, all aspects of the human potential previously discussed must resonate with a sense of dynamic quality and balance unshakable from outside influence, remaining steadfast and true within the self. I fully recognize that humanity in its present state does not exhibit the full potential of all the aspects we have discussed in this material. The challenge is great even for an individual–let alone a group of six billion people–to realize the human potential. I am not above any individual. Through this writing experience, as well as my own human experience, I, too, constantly strive to realize and maintain my human potential and to create and establish Balance in my own continuum.

There is nothing intrinsically wrong if one has not mastered every potential; I am here to offer opportunities and understanding to help you along the way. If we can each just learn to be kind to the self, we may find that we enjoy this journey of discovery called life to a greater extent than if we meandered through it ignorant of the possibilities that come with striving to reach our human potential.

The Ebb and Flow of Balance in a Relationship

A dynamic partner is not a completion, but rather a complement of oneself. If we move into relationships with the expectation that the other person will make us whole, that relationship will be destined for certain disappointment. I have always abhorred that line in the movie *Jerry Maguire* when Tom Cruise dramatically states, "You complete me." Certainly this would place a tremendous amount of pressure and accountability on the other to live up to this responsibility, and who could blame her if she went running in the opposite direction?

When we are "needy" of another and assign them the "job" of partner, we place considerable responsibility, pressure, and expectation on the relationship, for we are in constant worry that the other will not meet our requirements, thus causing us to lose sight of the opportunities that can be discovered in this union. This is not to say we must abandon each other in moments of need; however, we must come together needing nothing from one another, so that we may experience the grandness of the union, free of want and necessity. Of course, when our beloved experiences those moments when there is a cause for assistance, we do not abandon our partner, either; we create and maintain the Balance of the partnership in the very act of assistance. There can be a Balance in the need, as well, but it is when we are "needy" of each other that the scales begin to tip.

When we are in partnership with one another, of course those moments will come when it is necessary to lend assistance to our partner. When each partner in a relationship has achieved that Balance within the self first and foremost and the opportunity arises for one to offer assistance to the other, both magnificent parties will summon the strength of the Balance within the self and offer Balance to the other so that both parties, regardless of the situation, can move though the experience to reach a place of greater self wisdom.

This greater wisdom–knowing–of the individual self is an opportunity from the Universe that allows us to recall that greater part of the self as we interact and become co-creative with another.

ATTRACTION IS MAGNETIC

When we begin a partnership with a sense of completeness and individuality of the self, we are open to experience both opportunity with another and that which we may not have been able to have on our own. We journey to this amalgamation so that we may experience what it is we "become" when interacting with another, for in that interaction, we demonstrate qualities of the self not illustrated when we reside as an individual. We discover ourselves experiencing something greater than the whole of our individuality.

On the other hand, we may also discover through the relationship a negative aspect of the self, in other words, something that may not serve the greater good of the self. Once in the relationship, this dormant aspect can cause us, and our partner, to experience the worst possible part of the self. We may experience those moments because another can bring out the worst qualities of our selves. These seemingly negative traits already exist within our selves; otherwise it would not be possible for them to manifest.

I believe we come to that particular experience so those specific negative qualities can be made known to us, and perhaps, in conjunction with awareness, so we can redirect that energy into something positive. Some may choose to deny that such negativity can exist within the self; however, if that negativity did not already exist, it would not manifest itself. Somewhere in the fabric of the individual physical being, a quality must be encoded for it to demonstrate itself in physical form. This code is the energy of the human form as influenced by the planetary positions at the moment of birth. So through this human experience, we are at choice as to what we may experience at any given moment during any particular incarnation over the course of infinite time and space.

Some may pose the question: "Why is it that we attract certain types of individuals?" We often hear the term "opposites attract"; I would tend to disagree with that statement on the Metaphysical level. (A reminder, we are speaking in terms of Metaphysical understandings and concepts during this discussion.) There is a polarity when attracting another; however, within that *polarity* there needs to be a *similarity* in order for the two individual spirits to come together.

There is an analogous vibe that we radiate that attracts the similarity in another to bring that person to us. I learned a long time ago during my early days of metaphysical study–and I believe it was Mr. José Silva who posed the idea—that there are no accidents through-out the Universe, only coincidence. If what we would call an "accident" really were an accident, that would indicate imperfection in the Universe, suggesting all occurrences are haphazard. A "coincidence" coincides with a mutual attraction resonating from the etheric body, vibrating into the ether of the atmosphere sur-rounding the Earth—vibrating, radiating, moving dynam-ically through the air until it "catches" something simi-lar, bringing it to itself.

For example, a car "accident" is not really an acci-dent; we label it an accident because the action was not consciously intended to occur. In other words, we were unaware of the nature of the dynamic of the sequence of events that led to that incident. The events that may have led to the experience of that accident may have resonated out of the individual's thought process, stemming from an overabundance of misdi-rected thought energy that had been channeled improperly. This exemplifies only one of many possi-bilities creating such an outcome.

This may not be a common understanding, but as we progress into the coming years, I have great hopes for the advancement of humanity and know that we will come to a greater understanding of the human condition's vivaci-ty and its existence as a creative and dynamic force.

There is something electric within the human form. Brainwaves are electric, and there is electricity in the atmosphere, as demonstrated by lightning during a storm. So, isn't it possible that we can we send out electrical vibrations into the atmosphere? A simple example is when we give each other a shock caused by static electricity. As was discussed in chapter three about how our Thoughts create the realities in which we live, these electric "magnetic" thoughts bring forth specific types of individuals out of the energy that resonates within the etheric field, or aura, of the individual.

RELATIONS WITH LOVER/SPOUSE

The bond created with a lover or spouse is more intertwined than that of a platonic friend or business partner. There is a greater emotional intensity, depth of experience of the human condition, and a greater sense of vulnerability than we experience in contrast to other relationships. There is also the physical intimacy that exists within the structure of the romantic partnership, which, through the exchange of that particular dynamic energy–we will discuss sex in chapter eight–creates etheric bonds greater, deeper, and stronger than with a non-sexual relationship. Over long periods of time, the close proximity of the energy fields enables a constant interaction of the two eventually creating a mesh between the fabric of the etheric beings.

When an emotional relationship goes awry, it can be one of the most devastating and damaging experiences we have while in human form because the lattice of energy that has been created between these partners begins to fray. Regardless of our physical separation from any individual with whom we have some form of interaction, we will always have an etheric bond to the spirit, as is demonstrated by our connection to those who have moved before us into the spirit realm.

The bonds of the lover experience are formed at a level deeper than a relationship that is just superficial, and the interaction and the exchange of energy on the sexual level–which we will discuss in greater detail in the coming chapter–intertwines the connections much more profoundly. So, when the relationship has been exhausted, the results can be overwhelming. The essence of the self knows it has shared its particles with the other, just as the other has shared with the self, and so, perhaps, each fears the loss of that part of himself that may never be recovered, ultimately contributing to the mourning of the end of the union and the sense of devastation that may follow.

When for many months and years we share ourselves in the same bed with our lover, there is a mergence of the spirits during sleep. This dance of the spirits, beloveds hand in hand on the astral plane eloquently intertwining, is the intermingling of the pure essence (which we come to know as the soul) of each individual in the microcosm of the fibers of this being. Here, we are presented with the opportunity to truly become one in unification with our beloved. At this dimension, if the individual spirits are of a high vibration, there can be an experience free from the human condition, free from the arguments and distractions of everyday living, and free from the human form to experience a piece of Heaven with our lover that we can not experience in our waking state.

Yes, it is possible to have this experience with any other spirit as we experience sleep; however, with those whom we share both our waking and sleep experiences, there occurs a double exposure on the imprint of the relationship.

If one or both individuals is not of a high spiritual vibration, the negativity and toxicity of the relationship can be carried during sleep into the spirit dimension. We, as human beings, are not always completely free of negativity during sleep, especially if we share our spirit world with individuals who fervently resist releasing anything negative from their self. These negative conditions are transferred into the sleep dimension. This can be why we may experience the presence of someone in our dream state with whom we've shared an unresolved negative situation, even after many years of separation from the other. The dream may consist of an argument or a peaceful union giving solace to an unsettled situation. On some dimension, the individual's essence desires to create Balance where there may have been unresolved circumstances. This opportunity is not limited to those who remain with us in human form, but extends to those who have crossed into the spirit dimension.

Business as Usual?

The dynamics that one experiences in relationship with a business partner can differ considerably from those relations with a lover. For one, there is no physical intimacy. Usually. The goals are different in a business relationship than in other relationships, since we enter these unions with different desires. However, if we are to experience the full dynamic quality and opportunity of this union, the principles of Balance must also apply. There is the momentum to achieve a similar goal in this type of union, and the Balance is needed as well.

The typical business world as it is today seems to be one of the least evolved aspects of the human condition. This is not to say that great potential doesn't exist in the business realm, but there is lack of awareness of the opportunities presented to us when we operate in terms of "win/lose" and not "win/win." At the highest level of awareness, we are always at a place of win/win; we simply need to choose to see that opportunity.

If we were to move toward creating a business, regardless of what the enterprise may be, and truly establishing something of service to humanity, we would become aware that no matter what it is we choose to do, we are in a win/win situation. The Balance is established when we set our business goals to be for a purpose greater than just self-aggrandizement because then the positive energy will be returned to us. The Balance here is in the giving and receiving for services rendered. There is an imbalance when exorbitant amounts of compensation are being paid to individuals whose services are incongruent with that compensation. This may be allowed to carry on for a period of time, but unless the self creates a Balance, the Universe will see to it that Balance becomes restored. Either way, Balance will come about.

Let us review as an example the present condition of the United States and the circumstances of exorbitant and rising oil prices. Here in the U.S. we have seen oil prices skyrocket within a short period of time. The oil companies claim they are attempting to recoup their loss because of natural disasters such as 2005's Hurricane Katrina, which, incidentally, I predicted in December of 2004. However, in early 2006, it was reported in the media that in 2005 the major oil companies experienced record profits. I'm by no means an economist, but if these companies claimed hardship due to natural disasters such as Hurricane Katrina, how could they make record-breaking profits? Wouldn't some of those profits be needed to repair oil rigs damaged during the hurricane? Why would it be necessary for the government to give the people's tax money to the oil companies for repair compensation when their profits far exceeded the aid?

In this example, if the companies are, in fact, taking advantage of the population and these increases are not warranted, the Universe will see fit to create a Balance in this situation. The proper condition has occurred to present another opportunity for humanity to take control of its present condition and the course it's taking. I will elaborate more upon this matter in chapter twelve.

THE BALANCE OF NATURE

To quote Johann Wolfgang von Goethe: "So divinely is the world organized that every one of us, in our place and time, is in Balance with everything else." The essence of this chapter really is all about creating Balance–as well as beauty (once the Balance has been created)–in all aspects of our existence, and we may not be aware that Balance must be established in *all* areas of the human potential until we are faced with the challenge of creating Balance in a relationship.

I always defer to nature and I look up to the heavens whenever I am seeking truth or clarity about any situation. When there is an imbalance in nature, she will strive to create a Balance so that the harmony and perfection that innately exists can continue its growth and progression. When nature remains untouched by human hands and follows her own course, the resulting beauty is breathtakingly unique because Mother Nature herself painted the picture. When there is an imbalance in nature, if left to its own accord, nature will create a Balance to adjust and accommodate for the imbalance.

Unfortunately, we humans think we know better and thus interfere with nature's instinctive course. If it is so demonstrated in nature, and we humans are the highest

expression of intelligence, shouldn't we be able to manifest the same within our own lives?

An example in nature where beauty is created from
Balance is illustrated in the process of an oyster creating
a pearl. A beautiful pearl emerges from a state of imbalance within the oyster created by the simple presence of
a grain of sand. Once it is lodged within the mollusk, this
foreign matter quickly becomes an irritant. To heal that
irritation, the oyster's body reacts by depositing layers
of nacreous (pearl-like) substance around the foreign
object (the grain of sand) to wall it off and reduce irritation. The oyster is attempting to restore Balance within
its self from the imbalance that the foreign matter has
created. Through this process of creating Balance,
nature creates a thing of beauty: the pearl. We, too, as
human beings in Balance with nature possess the potential to create beauty in our humanness by establishing
Balance within ourselves.

LOVE AND BALANCE

When we began this section, we learned that in our
progression from the internal to the external self, we are
no longer individuals separate from each other in this
human condition. In order for us to experience a harmonious coexistence with one another, we must realize the
need for Balance within every union.

In chapter one, we came to know the self as a potential of the human experience; now, we have progressed

to the area of partnerships. With partnerships, we may experience the potential of creating the necessary Balance in all human experiences.

The human potential of the experience of a partnership–regardless of the manner in which the partnership may demonstrate itself–is that we are presented with the opportunity to experience ourselves in a manner that may not necessarily be available to us in our experience as individuals. The planetary energies of Venus and the sign Libra are associated with partnerships and Balance. Venus, the Goddess of Love and Beauty, thrives when given the opportunity to experience herself in unison with another. Libra's true quest is for Balance–perhaps the Balance that so delicately resides in nature–within the human condition. Perhaps if we sought each partnership experience as a loving union, we might find a sense of harmony. I always felt that if we greeted our co-workers with a hug every day, there would be a drastically different sense of dynamic that would resonate throughout the day because this beauty and Balance are as necessary in our business interactions as they are on the personal level.

eight

Transformation

There are as many nights as days, and the one is just as long as the other in the year's course. Even a life cannot be without a measure of darkness, and the word "happy" would lose its meaning if it were not balanced by sadness. It is far better to take things as they come along with patience and equanimity.
—CARL JUNG

Throughout life, we experience seasons that are known in metaphysical studies as "The Dark Night of the Soul." This is a necessary "evil" in life if one is to experience the spiritual, etheric being that is the essence of the true self. This experience offers us the opportunity to progress along the evolutionary scale of spirituality by releasing the past and its situations that are no longer of service. In order for the individual to move forward without the limitations of past events, the individual must experience "dark times" as an opportunity to reinvent his human potential.

Like any challenging experience during our human existence, the time of darkness is only temporary, for if we are to revel in the Light, we must also experience dark times. This outwardly dark period needn't be seen as something negative or pointless if we take the time to review the experience for its value and seek out its benefits for our humanness.

Pluto, the planet sometimes referred to as the Dark Knight, is associated with obscure issues and shadowy times, transitions and transformations, and the reinvention of the self. Pluto rules the zodiac sign Scorpio, known for its intensity, darkness, and deep, murky waters. We must navigate through the sludge and shadows with patient faith if we are to experience any type of rebirth.

Pluto's distance from the Sun and the Earth allows it to remain in the shadows, thus creating a mysticism that surrounds this dark planet and providing an explanation as to why it is often misunderstood. Because of its distance from the Earth, its energy is extremely subtle yet magnificent in complexity and strength when it does show itself. Usually, it can seem that Pluto is apathetic to Universal proceedings; he just floats around the solar system ticking off the days as they pass. However, when his time arrives, his power is a force to be reckoned with. Once Pluto takes us by the hand and we experience the transformation he stimulates in us, we realize that his effects are truly understated and long lasting, and we are never quite the same for it.

One example of this, and this scenario is extremely similar to what we may go through during a life-challenging experience, is when the soul prepares for its departure and begins the process of detaching itself from the physical body. The soul–which I define as that essence of who we truly are that is a part of the All That Is–is ending its journey here on the Earth plane, so it no longer requires the physical body as its vessel. Housing itself within a physical body no longer serves any purpose. The physical body is heavy, filled with thick matter; in a way, this form encumbers the soul, which has finished its journey on Earth. The time has come for it to free itself from that which no longer serves its purpose, leaving behind its exercise in "forgetfulness of Light" to move back into the Light of the All That Is.

The soul is not reluctant to remove itself from the body, for it knows the freedom it can and will experience now that it has exhausted its time in the body. When, in our physical humanness, we are not enlightened–in touch with our soul–we find it difficult to embark on the journey of departure from our Earthly experience, to accept the death of our physical incarnation.

In life, we often catch ourselves reacting the exact same way during a time of transition. We refuse to let go of the familiar, even when the necessity to do so is obvious. We enjoy the comfort of what we know and are reluctant, often fearful, to look within the shadows of the uncertain future. However, if we seek out the Universal Light, allow it to illuminate what is shadowed in darkness, the reality that we see may not appear as dismal as we feared.

Just as the literal light of the Full Moon illuminates the darkness of the night, so does the lunar cycle slowly bring a shimmer of figurative light to illuminate the shadowy, unclear areas of life. As the light of the Moon grows during its waxing phase, we become aware that the obscurity in our life is really an illusion. The Full Moon's culmination also encourages fruitful progress in our endeavors. Ultimately, the light of day (the Sun) and the light of the Moon equally render dark places less frightening, for the Light of the All That Is will always bring one to a place of clarity and awareness whenever that Light has been given an opportunity to shine.

This period of the Dark Night of the Soul is simply a time of clarity, transition, and Transformation. Some may see their entire Earthly experience as a time of Darkness because not only have they forgotten the Light that radiates from their essence, which was never extinguished, but they also never make the choice to remember their Light until their souls depart the physical bodies. In the end, the reality is that the Light is never really switched off; it's simply forgotten in the blink of an eye–the time it takes to begin the Earthly experience–and remains forgotten until the spirit, the soul, chooses to see it again.

In order for the soul to go into the Light, it must release itself from what is no longer of service. This experience for some, whether during the process of change *or* death, may be one of reluctance, for the being may not become aware of the transition until it has, quite literally, gone kicking and screaming through the process and come out the other side all the better for the experience. And still there are others who choose to remain forever in limbo, fearing the solace of the Light. Then there are those beings who have left their physical body, unaware that they have embarked upon this transition to the next dimension, for they are reluctant and refuse to let go of the familiarity of the Earthly experience.

During the Sun's transit of the sign of Scorpio from approximately October 20/21 to November 20/21, some celebrate the Pagan festival Samhain (chiefly in the Northern hemisphere), which is pronounced *sow-EN* and, incidentally, is another name for Halloween. Throughout history, the midpoint of the sign of Scorpio was usually the mark of this particular celebration, since the midpoint of most any object is the strongest point.

When the trees surrender their leaves to the autumn winds and nature transitions to a time of darkness, this is also when the days become their shortest and the light of the day is not always as bright. This time of year can be very similar to this experience of the Dark Night of the Soul. If we, as humans, would be as graceful as the trees that surrender their cloak of leaves in the autumn when it is time for us to surrender that which we hold onto so intently–be it as grand as laying down our

Earthly life or as worldly as changing careers—and advance to life's next station, our return to Light may not seem so dismal. Just as we celebrate the return to light in December (each successive winter day experiences an increasing duration of sunlight from the previous), so, too, should we celebrate the dark, for it returns us to the remembrance of Light. As with all things, it is always our choice to accept the transformation and then return to the Light.

THE BEGINNINGS OF CHANGE

If we are to advance in our life's journey, it is necessary to experience a grand metamorphosis brought about by the Dark Night of the Soul. Like the chrysalis that acts as a bridge between the transformation of caterpillar to butterfly, there are moments during our life when we encounter a similar transition, but we must allow the self to make the choice to surrender to the experience.

The caterpillar is aware when the time has come for its miraculous transformation. We, too, as humans, would do well to acknowledge when the time of transition is necessary during this Earthly experience. The caterpillar moves into a period of seeming gloom (its time in the chrysalis), just as some of us do during these dark times, where it lies sleeping in its cocoon. During that time of seeming gloom, however, it really is not sleeping, but rather undergoing one of nature's most wondrous transitions. We, too, have the ability to experience the same metamorphosis in our lives.

This is not to say this period is not one of great struggle for the caterpillar. As it emerges from its cocoon, it must be diligent to extricate itself from the cloak (cocoon) that no longer serves its existence, similar to the human who must shed his past experiences as he comes out of his period of darkness. The butterfly must summon strength and stamina to break through its husk and emerge with poise and beauty. Despite this difficult and exhausting process, the tiny creature seems to rise effortlessly to the challenge. Innately it knows that this is the only path to growth, to its own evolution. Can we not do the same?

Within each individual there exists some form of willpower and determination; we must choose to demonstrate that pre-existing quality within the self to make it real in the physical world. The depth and darkness of Pluto also pertain to the existence of one's willpower. This opportunity, this time for self-reinvention, is a time when the falseness of the self is stripped away, allowing the truth of the self to radiate.

REBIRTH, REGENERATION, REVIVIFICATION

If we do not experience this process of reinvention, the soul-self will remain stagnant in the human condition and the experience will be in vain. A rebirthing process at various times in our lives helps us to grow and progress as spiritual beings on the ethereal level. A periodic cleansing of that which does not serve us may ease the process of transformation when the time is at hand. We will have less clutter to discard when the time comes to move forward and progress to the next station in our existence.

For instance, if we routinely do a spring cleaning of our physical home, discarding what may be useless or unnecessary, when the time comes for us to move to another location, the transition will be easy, as there will be little clutter to pack and move. As I stated in chapter four, tremendous clutter in the home is a reflection of the clutter that has been accumulating in the fibers of an individual's aura. Elimination of that clutter on a periodic basis would make the travel experience much lighter–literally!

As we trek through this human experience over many years, we accumulate, collect, squirrel away–this can pertain to both material things and the people we encounter in our lives. This also includes heavy and negative thoughts that are no longer of service to the self. As time passes, it is in our best interest to rid ourselves of these obsolete possessions rather than carry them with us from season to season. What may have been of value when we were 21 may not hold the same usefulness or benefits at age 42.

We are creatures of habit, not always willing to change. This is not intended as a judgment, simply an observation of human behavior that is neither right nor wrong; however, would you wear the same and only pair of shoes for ten years after walking thousands of miles in them? There comes a point when those shoes have holes and are not only uncomfortable, but likely doing physical damage to your feet, legs, hips, and back. Though it is not necessarily wrong for you to continue wearing those shoes, does it really serve your best interest?

ENDING OF AN ERA

Change and transformation are mandatory if we choose to continue the growth of the soul while progressing along this physical Earthly experience. When we encounter moments that force us to review and evaluate situations evoking painful emotions and difficult decisions, we enter a period when we must reinvent ourselves. This cycle of transformation allows us to adjust to new conditions and circumstances, which is essential for us to survive in a manner congruent with the true self. This may happen at 28; it may happen at 78. The choice to surrender to the experience, as always, is ours. When we do choose to surrender and allow the great God of Transformation to take us by the hand and lead us forward, the process is much easier.

This God of Transition is, of course, Pluto. He is the Great Dark One, but not one of evil, as the word "dark" sometimes implies. Quite simply, he helps uncover the truth–the genuineness of what we truly are on the soul's level. This misunderstood force assists us with the great realization of the self. Pluto reminds the self of its mortality and our finite years in this dimension of consciousness. He brings us to a time of opportunity so that we may reassess and reinvent the self and continue on this journey with a sense of newness and vitality, regardless of our physical age.

The Balance created in this section, which is founded in the characteristics discussed in chapter two, deals with the truth, or more precisely, the realization of false truth and false idolatry that may no longer serve our existence. In chapter two, we learned of the need to create material things, the adornments of the human condition. Here, we now realize that those things are no longer necessary; we must let go of the false reverence we have placed on those things. This is when we learn the truth: to move up on the evolutionary spiral, we must regenerate by allowing the unnecessary material things to dissolve away, thus making room for the things that are more in line with the new self. If those things that enhanced our life, as mentioned in chapter two, no longer serve a greater purpose to the self, we must choose to recognize that truth, then release–give freedom to–that which no longer serves its purpose.

We may find ourselves progressing through the years with a sense of uncertainty about who we are–or perhaps who we "think" we are. These ideas may not be our own; they may have been instilled within us during our early development. They may likely comprise notions defining who we should be, and just as likely not be an accurate description of the essence of who we are. Or, perhaps, we create our lives as we think we are "supposed" to live them.

In order for us to have an accurate, conscious understanding of the truth of who we really are on the soul's level, we must come out of the darkness and embrace the Light. Through all Transformations on this Earthly existence, we are presented with the opportunity to reach the awareness of this Light.

The manner in which we reinvent ourselves at different times in our lives is completely our choice; however, it sometimes seems as though the Universe threw us a curve ball when we review the circumstances surrounding a particular experience.

At different points in life, events occur that force us to re-evaluate who we are and then adapt. This may seem like external conditions are out of our control; however, as with all things in the Universe, no event can transpire unless the spirits of all individuals involved are in agreement. The Universe does not acknowledge the difference between the killer and his victim. When the essence of both individual spirits reside on a higher level of consciousness, both will review, without human judgment, why those events occurred. And through those experiences, both individuals, who are actually part of the Universal whole, will have evolved in a manner unique and specific to the essence of their being.

THE ASPECTS OF THE TRANSITION

Once we have journeyed through the aforementioned transition, we will notice unmistakable changes in the fiber of our being, both at the soul's level and in the human form. We are never really quite the same after a transition of great magnitude transpires within us.

From an intellectual standpoint, we will find ourselves thinking with great clarity and consistency, finally harmonious with the truth of our being. And we will be free of thoughts that did not serve the purpose of our being, thoughts that had become instilled on an unconscious level simply because of our surroundings and the influence of our experience. When these obsolete, distracting thoughts are released from the psyche, the mind is finally free from views that are no longer truly representative of the self.

From an emotional standpoint, changes take place during this transition that allow us a greater understanding of the depth of our being. The emotional condition becomes more refined, and we comprehend more clearly the complexity of our humanness.

From a physical standpoint, some may experience great changes to the body, occasionally even verging on unrecognizable metamorphosis. For example, one may experience a significant reduction in body weight simply because everything that was inefficient is no longer present, including the original cause of the weight gain. The body may find itself operating at a higher, or even optimal, performance level, efficiently eliminating unnecessary toxins from the body. The excess baggage, if you will, is no longer an issue; the body now processes its fuel more efficiently.

And finally, the spiritual aspect of this transition finds the soul–the true essence of the being–returning to and remembering the Light. Once again, Light can encompass the human form that transports the soul through its journey of life, but now with a dynamic that is much more at peace and harmony with the soul's existence.

PHYSICAL DEATH OF A LOVED ONE

When we experience the death of someone close to us, this transformative phase of life is thrust upon us. We are forced to face our own mortality, to reassess life, and to acknowledge its limits in terms of the physical. (Just to remind you, when I speak of death, I'm referring only to the end of the physical body, for our soul continues on *ad infinitum*.) In death, the physical body is no longer present; however, the true essence of that self is revealed because the mask, if you will, is no longer part of the soul-self. The excess has been stripped away, the baggage eliminated, the burden of the body eradicated; all that remains is the lightness of the soul's true fundamental nature in the Universal continuum. The consequence of transition and transformation is as significant in life as it is in death. The same virtues transpire in a life-altering event to the self as those the soul experiences in a life-ending event.

The death of one close to us can ultimately lead us to

reassess the beliefs and philosophies that I will discuss in the coming chapter. We may find that through this experience comes a necessity to adjust the thought process in order to understand what has occurred. What may have held true in the past in regard to our thoughts and perspectives may no longer hold true once we experience this transformative process. Again, we must adjust and adapt. If we were to continue along the same line of thinking at 40 as we did at 21, we would find that we never really progressed to a higher place of the self.

I Want Your Sex

I'm not certain we could discuss any matter pertaining to our human potential without discussing sex.

The experience of the sexual energy exchange creates a bond between two individuals that is more entwined than that of a platonic friend or acquaintance. Although, if there were a sexual exchange between friends or acquaintances, then these ideas would apply to those instances, as well. In this section, I will sometimes refer to sex as an energy exchange that results in a transformative experience, for after a sexual encounter, do we not feel transformed?

When two individuals are in the throes of this sexual energy exchange, an interconnectivity of the lower chakras (energy points) of the etheric being develops. This becomes increasingly intensified and solidified over the course of this lover experience.

Once the relationship has been exhausted, this etheric bond of sexual energy is still very much intact. If this relationship is no longer fruitful to both individuals and each has progressed to a place where they no longer share this energy exchange dance, a separation of this energy must occur. This could be why there are unpleasant difficulties in severing a relationship that is no longer of service. Though we may no longer be physical with the other, these etheric cords continue to connect both individuals on the etheric level. "Cutting" these etheric cords through the process of visualization and meditation will ease this process of separation. (If you're interested in learning more about cutting etheric cords, a good place to start might be Doreen Virtue's *Angel Medicine: How to Heal the Body and Mind with the Help of the Angels*.)

THE POWER OF SEX

The correlation in this section between sex, power, and Transformation stems from the characteristics of the planet of sex and power, Pluto, and the sign of Scorpio. The energy qualities of a sexual encounter are so powerful that some may choose to bastardize that power for manipulation. Pluto equals great power, as does sex. Just as when the great power-potential of Pluto is misdirected, causing doomed and destructive outcomes, so, too, can the misdirected power of sexual energy cause equal disruptions.

When Pluto's full power-potential is released in a negative manner (negative, as in an action that does not serve a greater purpose), the destructive results can be equated to the power released in an atomic explosion. (Incidentally, Pluto rules atomic energy, nuclear devices, and the process of nuclear fission created as a result of an atomic or nuclear detonation.) I use this analogy to provide you with a complete understanding of the power potential of Pluto's energies.

The above is an extreme example of the misuse of Pluto's energy. The release of sexual energy exhibits similar qualities, metaphorically, when observed as a release of energy from the body. It transforms the physical being, creating a biological alteration in the body that results in a feel-good sensation. This is very similar to the biological sensations created when one overindulges in food with the fruitless hope of filling the seeming emptiness within the self.

Sexual energy becomes negative when it is misused to manipulate in order to gain something from another by any means that does not correlate with the true essence of the other. This energy comes from a dark place within the self, and when one chooses to control and manipulate in order to achieve his desires, he proves himself to be "in the dark" about the essence of his true self and of the other.

Another aspect of sex is that it can be used as a means of gaining emotional security. We discussed in chapter two about how we might gain a sense of security by amassing material objects. In this chapter, the example would be someone believing the long-held misconception that he can fulfill his need for emotional security through the exchange of sexual energy. As with all things, emotional security must resonate from the Foundations of the self that was covered in chapter four. One cannot find emotional security through the power of sex, just as one person cannot "complete" another, as I mentioned in chapter seven.

When one intends to enter into a sexual act to exchange and transfer his spirit energy with another and that act is based solely on his own desires, he should reconsider why he is pursuing the sexual act. Sexual power is best when shared with spirits who mutually seek the energy transference.

And please don't be mistaken by assumptions. This dark sexual energy is not exclusive to violent sexual behavior. It can be something as simple as a man who has no desire to pursue a long-term relationship making a conscious decision to mislead a woman who he knows desires marriage by saying that he wants the same things she does just so he can have sex with her. When the tryst is done, he leaves her feeling upset and misused. (Actually, it's not as simple as I first mentioned.) Now imagine if this one tryst leads to an unexpected, unwanted pregnancy. Complications abound when just one person acts from a place of shadows. Instead of this sexual exchange resulting in a release of accumulated energy, both of these parties have now accumulated new, problematic (negative/dark) energy.

THE BEGINNING OF THE KNOWING

As we experience these transformative times throughout our Earthly journey, we reach a point of insight. We say to ourselves, "Oh yes, that's it...now it makes sense!" We suddenly realize that all along we've already known everything that we need to know. It's all there and available for the taking once we choose to invite that "knowing," that Light, into the physical realm. As I mentioned earlier in this book, all that is, was, and will be has been recorded in the great Book of Records. All we need to do is tap into this recollection and bring to form the solutions to whatever may seem impossible.

Certainly the Universe would not have allowed the soul-self to embark upon this Earthly journey without the necessary tools for survival. As we progress unto this New Age with a greater understanding of the tools of meditation, astrological and psychic knowledge, and a convergence into oneness with nature, these answers will seem more obvious to human beings.

THE BEGINNING IS THE END, THE END IS THE BEGINNING

The experience of Transformation can be closely equated to the experience we have now come to know as Death. However, this transference of energy is not the end, but rather a continuation of the whole of the soul's progress and evolution. Just as the soul experiences the dropping of the physical body because it is no longer of service to the soul, we will, in fact, encounter similar transitional periods in life when we find ourselves dropping what is no longer of service to us and moving forward with the human experience in a manner that was not possible beforehand.

This is equated with the energies of the Great Transformer, our far-distant friend Pluto, and his counterpart, Scorpio. Because of his great distance from our Earthly home, the vibrations of this heavenly body are very, very subtle, yet extremely powerful and, at times, explosive. Whenever we come into contact with this seemingly ominous planet, our lives are forever changed. Nothing is quite the same once we have traveled through the Dark Night of the Soul and have once again emerged like the Phoenix from the ashes and returned to Light.

This process of transition is of great necessity if we are to have an Earthly experience that is evolutionary to the progress of the soul. Just as the power of Pluto transforms the self on many levels, so, too, can the exchange of sexual energy transform the spirit-self vibration. This exchange of sexual energy, if done in Light, provides each of us with the opportunity for the Soul-self to release itself of energy that has been accumulated.

nine
Beliefs, Philosophy, and the Psyche

The best theology would need no advocates: it would prove itself.
–KARL BARTH

In chapter three, we discussed how, through the process of our thoughts, we create and construct our personal reality and how those thoughts affect and modify that reality. This chapter is the higher octave of what we touched upon in that section. We will review how our expanding thoughts begin to affect our perception of the world, as well as how we influence it. From these newly expanding thoughts and insights, we begin to form our philosophical assessment of the world around us. We also discover how the thoughts that created our personal realities are now also creating the realities and the existing condition of the Global Village.

In this chapter, the influence radiates from the planet of great expansion, Jupiter, and the sign of the zodiac that it rules, Sagittarius, the philosopher of the zodiac. Sagittarius is also the priest and the prophet and provides opportunity for spiritualism. We will also review how those personal thoughts have an effect on a global scale while in co-creation with the collective unconscious.

Within the continuum of the planet's atmosphere resides the collective unconscious level where our thoughts travel, literally roving around the world in seconds! Just as radio waves, transmissions from cell phones, and television and satellite signals travel around the world, so, too, do our thoughts. Those electromagnetic impulses in the brain–which, in my understanding, is our Earthly connection to the pulse of the Universe–vibrate, radiate, emanate just like the transmissions of the aforementioned Earthly devices. Is it not yet obvious how we are influencing the creation and the condition of the world through our thoughts, words, and actions?

This wondrous place called Earth, which is a magnificent display of nature's majestic beauty, is, like us humans, a living, breathing, brilliant organism. The trees act as the lungs for the Earth, breathing in and filtering out toxins and impurities from the atmosphere so that we, its inhabitants, have an abundance of clean, fresh, oxygen to breathe, enabling us to co-exist with this wondrous organism. Just as the human body consists mostly of water, so, too, does our planet. And just as the Moon has influence over the ebb and flow of the Earth's ocean tides, so, too, does that same Moon, as do all the Heavenly bodies, have influence over the ebb and flow of the Human form.

A COMING OF AGE

As we progress through this human experience, we develop our own beliefs and philosophies about our personal perceptions of the world we inhabit. We examine our thoughts about the realities that we've created and we postulate how the reality we've constructed can fit into the greater whole: does it contribute a positive influence to the progress of both the self and humanity? This process is part of the continuation of co-creation with the Universe–how our thoughts are part of the whole of existence, demonstrating the reality that we are all part of the oneness of the All That Is.

For most of Humanity, this stage is reached somewhere in adulthood–though some may demonstrate these sophisticated abilities during their early years. The dynamics to become philosophical and a seeker of truth emerge from the experience of the human condition and the interaction of the self with humanity over the course of approximately 40-42 years. Some would call this stage of life the "Midlife crisis." At this period in life's journey, we may find ourselves breaking away from things in the past that no longer serve the greater purpose. We may notice, for example, that a job we have performed for the majority of our adult life is no longer satisfying and fulfilling. We are drawn into a journey to discover new and greater possibilities for a career, and, ultimately, for ourselves.

On the astrological level, we do not reach the milestone of adulthood until we are 28-29 years old, which marks our passage through all the stages of the life experience that prepare us for adulthood. So, the mid-life period is the next milestone, marking the time when we may find ourselves breaking away from those past experiences that have essentially influenced our existence but no longer serve it. The perceived notions of personal and global reality that come into play during these years are more profound and influential than if they were to take place at any other time during the life experience.

Fly the Ocean in a Silver Plane...

Traveling to those places far from our birthplace gives us the opportunity to become expansive in our thoughts, perceptions, and awareness–particularly of the realities of the everyday life. We have the chance to experience life as it exists outside the sphere of our familiar reality. If our Earthly experience does not allow us to see first-hand how people outside our home–be it in another town, state, region, or country–create their own existence, we will be constrained in our attempt to imagine the unification of humanity on a global scale. Limiting our experiences outside the home can hinder our perception of the realities of the life experience far across the globe. Henry David Thoreau summarized it perfectly:

> We boast of our system of education, but why stop at schoolmasters and schoolhouses? We are all schoolmasters and our schoolhouse is the universe. To attend chiefly to our desk or schoolhouse while we neglect the scenery in which it is placed is absurd.

Over many years, I traveled to far away places such as Singapore, Dubai, and Australia, as well as to many European countries. I've had the grand pleasure of experiencing such cities as Paris, Rome, and London, among dozens of others. As time passed, my perceptions of this world in which we live drastically and permanently changed. Through my appreciation for the diversity of the peoples and cultures in these lands so far from my home, I have come to realize that we, as humans, are not very different from each another. Through this observation, let us recognize that oneness of the All That Is that has been encoded in each of us.

It is a truly humbling experience to be presented with the opportunity to dwell in a country so far from home. To live among the people, adapt to the culture of the land, sample exotic foods, even dress as those of the region can be an eye-opening experience.

Visiting other lands far from the familiarity of our everydayness affords us the opportunity to expand our minds. As I stated, one of the traits of Jupiter is the ability to expand our realities. Since this chapter is the higher octave of chapter three, the experience of far-away travel grants our thought perceptions the opportunities to expand beyond our home and out into the world beyond. The result: our personal, newly developed thoughts intertwine with the philosophies of the collective unconscious of this world, allowing the creation of a greater reality.

VALUES

Each time before we enter this Earthly existence from the spirit world, we establish certain conclusions about the sort of values–morals–we will choose to demonstrate while progressing through the given incarnation in this time-space continuum. I will refer to this as our Ethereal Value Imprint (EVI) for matters of this discussion.

While we roamed the spirit world before entering into a union with the physical body, we dwelled among our spirit comrades, we pondered about the potential of the experiences we would undertake while in human form, and we chose the precise moment and geographical location on planet Earth when we would take our first breath of this Earthly experience.

I firmly hold this to be my truth: we choose the moment when we will unite with the physical form. The planetary energies encoded in our being at that moment give us the colors for the palette with which we paint this Earthly experience. Our conscious choice is the picture we choose to create while living on Earth. Free will is *always* at hand; we are always at choice as to how we create, respond to, and re-create our Earthly realities and experiences.

This truth is reality if we only choose to see it. When we find ourselves "blaming" others for the condition of our lives, accusing whatever deity we feel is responsible for the mishap and misfortune in our reality, we are choosing to play the role of victim rather than to be accountable and responsible for our thoughts, words, and actions. We are demonstrating our lack of awareness about our selves and humanity.

As we move through the journey of life, sometimes we learn our values and other times our EVI kicks in and overrides what we have been taught. For example, why is it that ultra-liberal parents can raise a child who may ultimately grow up to be ultra-conservative? There is nothing intrinsically wrong with either point of view, but it is curious how this divergence occurs. What is of greater service to the self is how we evaluate that learned principle. With spiritual awareness, we have the ability to determine whether or not what we have been taught is congruent with how we choose to experience and create our lives. If it is, we will make the choice to continue creating our existence with those values. If it is not, we must choose, with awareness, to seek out that which is compatible with our own personal beliefs and philosophies of the world. If it feels right, then it is your truth.

Part of the remembrance of the essence of the True Self throughout this Earthly experience might be how we radically break away from what we were educated and instructed to believe–and have faith in–throughout our formative years. I, for one, have a conglomeration of planets in the sector of my chart that deals with all the ideologies we are discussing here. Through my Earthly experiences, I have developed understandings and truths about my own spirituality and the interplay of humanity that are far removed from anything instilled within me as a child.

The choice to persevere through childhood and eventually hypothesize my own personal truths of humanity, spirituality, and the oneness of the All That Is was by my conscious volition. I chose to formulate my personal conclusions about this physical world, as well as matters of spirituality and religious institutions. Though some may consider my conclusions to be "wrong" or "right," they are actually neither, as my conclusions relate to the experiences of my Self while journeying this Earth. These are the truths and realities of my humanly being; they may not fit into the model of someone else's experiences, but they are perfect for my Earthly presence as it relates to the model of the world I have come to know as my own.

WE PERCEIVE WHAT WE BELIEVE

There comes a point in our life's journey where we re-evaluate and reformulate our personal beliefs and belief system according to our life's experiences, as I mentioned in the prior passages. Some of us either choose to embrace the religious/philosophical belief system from childhood or begin to question and reframe that belief system as influenced by our personal experiences. Throughout this writing, I choose to use the term spirituality as a substitute for religion, for I feel our experience here is one of a spiritual journey–one that is unique and specific to when the individual is born unto a specific moment along the space-time continuum and how the individual interacts with the Spirit dimension. In discussing this aspect of the human potential, the focus is on the individual's personal spirituality and how that spirit's behavior creates ripples unto the world, influencing the collective unconscious like a pebble cast into a pond.

In our early years of development, we are instructed what to believe in terms of faith, religion, or a specific belief system. For the most part, we accept what we are taught and receive those teachings as truth–in reality, they are not "the" truth, but an aspect of "a" truth. Perhaps, as we progress as a whole, we may consider imparting to our younger generation all the varied belief systems that exist in the world. In some way, isn't each belief system in our world somehow linked to the core values of another belief system, thus all of them actually being a part of the greater whole belief value system?

If we show our future generations the beauty and possibilities of all belief and philosophy systems of the world around them, perhaps, in their own wisdom, they will come to know what best fits their personal models of the world in which they have been born. With hopeful consequence, they will take the religious, secular, or philosophical beliefs learned as children and synthesize them into a spiritual foundation, for when we entered this world, we actually embarked upon a spiritual journey and not a religious one. Spirituality is that part of the higher self that exists as truth; religion is something human-made. Spirituality is multifaceted, forever changing and evolving, the unification of the ceaselessly developing oneness of the spirit itself.

We can choose to re-solidify childhood religious beliefs or perhaps reformulate and restructure those beliefs or completely abandon them and create a customized belief system. Again, the choice is ours according to the path we have chosen to follow. No one path is wrong, only different.

Just Call Me Inspiration

Inspiration is the kindling, the spark, the very beginnings of a thought process that opens up perceptions into the many possibilities of our lives. Dr. Wayne Dyer once wrote, "God comes to us in the space between our thoughts." This is what I consider true inspiration. It is what comes to us when we get our thoughts out of the way, or, another way of putting it, when we release the ego. Inspiration is the messages from the universe, the highest creative intervention of divinity in the thought process. This is when Divine Intervention is permitted to influence the creative thought process.

The significance of inspiration is that it gives us greater

opportunity than our limited thoughts possibly could. It allows us to be creatively dynamic—a more refined creativity that possesses depth and profundity—when we permit ourselves to be. Inspiration opens the mind to greater possibilities beyond what the mind might perceive and conceive.

How many times over the course of our lives do we experience a jolt of inspiration only to dismiss it and cast it back into the sea of thoughts? This book is the manifestation of one of those thoughts, one that I could have easily dismissed as nonsense; however, in my intuitive knowingness, I realized this was a journey I needed to embark upon for myself, and hopefully to benefit humanity.

Through the years, I pondered over the many ideas that came to me about books I would create, but I was uncertain which one to develop first. (A bounty of ideas and concepts fills my journals, and I will nurture and release them in the coming years, each one in its appropriate time.) I had not yet experienced that bolt of inspiration powerful enough to move me to engage with the All That Is to begin this hallowed venture.

Then during 2005, I was enjoying a warm, mid-summer evening at an outdoor concert. I have always taken great pleasure in music as it is a great muse for my self—music truly is the inspiration of the soul. I was "lost" in my pleasure of the moment, my mind and thoughts somewhere in space, when I very gently, yet specifically, heard the name of this book and its entire structure in a stretch of time that seemed endless yet lasted only a nanosecond! This was inspiration, pure and divine, sharing with my higher self in a moment when my spirit and psyche were in tune with the cosmic vibration of the All That Is in the Universe.

I could have chosen to dismiss this idea as rubbish; however, there was something within me that possessed an etheric wisdom that declared this to be part of my journey. I could not ignore this knock on the spectral door to my spirit. Now, as I sit and write these words, there is divine presence surrounding me; I can feel the electromagnetic energy pulsing through my spirit, almost possessing me as the words simply come to and gently move through me.

I acknowledge that most of this ambitious journal has literally been channeled through the essence of my being from a place much higher than where my physical body resides.

DIVINE INSPIRATION OR EARTHLY DERIVATIVE

There are many times when ideas come to us that may seem far-fetched, out of the ordinary, seemingly obscure; we may dismiss those ideas as nonsense. At the onset, they may seem invalid; however, if there is something resonating within us from one of those ideas, a tingling sensation in the essence of our being, we may be receiving Divine intervention of inspiration—as was my own experience of intervention regarding the notion of this book!

When we permit ourselves to nourish and cultivate those ideas and allow them to take their organic path, we will find ourselves experiencing the manifestation of something amazing. And yes, there may be times when some ideas are not Divine Inspiration, but rather a multitude of excessive mental activity that can manifest itself simply from an overabundance of activity stemming from our daily lives. In other words, this faux inspiration is actually energy that has not been channeled and directed in a positive manner. It does not produce an outcome that is creative and dynamic but instead fabricates a clutter of excess mental activity and debris. And this noisy energy is a result of our Earthly experiences mucking up our Divine connections.

PSYCHIC FACULTIES

Intuition is an aspect of "knowing" that we will discuss in the final portion of my discourse of the human potential. Trusting the "gut" instinct that I commented on in chapter four is also a quality of this intuitive knowingness. All these qualities progress to the human potential culmination that will manifest in chapter twelve.

Within every human individual is instilled the eminence we recognize as psychic faculties (abilities)—quite simply, being "psychic," which originates from the Greek word *psychikos* meaning "of the soul." So, if this psychic quality is of the soul and within the essence of each individual exists the energy presence of the soul, then each and every one of us does, in fact, possess the talent to demonstrate psychic abilities. To tap into that talent, all we need to do is simply choose to demonstrate those abilities.

If one were to possess some potential talent or faculty that another does not (I am referring to how the human form has been created by the Universe), it would imply that the Universe creates conditions exclusive to each individual. And as I previously discussed, the Universe does not play favorites. Yes, there are those who have greater potential to demonstrate certain faculties, as was composed in their personal planetary composition; however, those same faculties exist somewhere within each individual's planetary configuration. Prior to unification with the physical body, one essence may have concluded that the contribution she would make to humanity when arriving on this plane would be to demonstrate a heightened sense of this faculty. And so begins her unique demonstration of those faculties.

ANGELS CALLING...

We have all experienced those moments when the phone rings and we just know who is calling. Or when driving home from the office, we divert from our usual route for some seemingly unknowing reason, only to discover later that a massive automobile accident occurred on our usual route and we likely would have been involved had we not made the unconscious change. This coincidental choice of action allowed us to avoid a situation that may have been disastrous.

So why, you might ask, would an individual have this intuitive "knowing" for one event but not for another that might actually avoid some life-altering, or even threatening, result? It is my understanding that each individual does, in fact, have the potential to demonstrate these abilities. These qualities make themselves known to some of us "naturally" and to others of us only after much mental discipline and determination.

When we are of a clear mind, free of unnecessary distractions and mental anguish, this "help from the other side" can come through to each of us. And again, we must choose it and *allow* it to be so. If an individual is driving home from the office and his mind is muddled with the day's chatter and burdened by the endless loop-tape of events that transpired on that day, the message may not come through loud and clear. The driver may have sensed the thought "maybe I should go this way today," but dismissed inspiration's message because other cluttered thoughts overruled the insight. I will even take it one step further; if the driver is involved in the mishap, perhaps that experience is meant to play an important part in that one's life. And if that's so, then the driver must choose to see the greater purpose of the event rather than just as a single annoying and unfortunate situation; if not, the event will have been for naught.

These psychic faculties embedded within each individual are at our disposal if we make that choice to use them.

Herein Lies the Prophets and the Prophecies

In this dimension of the human potential, we have discussed the higher level of the thought process as it relates to the greater part of the consciousness of humanity. The massive planet Jupiter, also known as the Great Expander because of his monstrosity, brings forth opportunities to develop and expand upon the individual's beliefs and belief system and incorporate the essence of those qualities into spirituality. Sagittarius, whom Jupiter rules, is symbolized by the Archer/Centaur always aiming his bow and arrow to the heavens in search of truth and wisdom.

Like the old, wise wizard as he progresses on his life's journey, we become philosophical in our thoughts about the personal realities we have created and how that reality conforms to the greater whole of humanity. The experience traveling to unfamiliar, far-off lands expands the mind to accept greater possibilities of a superior reality. We learn to visualize a world that can exist that can be grander than we were ever able to imagine before we traveled outside the realm of our hometown.

Through the instincts and intuition rising from the psychic faculties, divine intervention of Inspiration has the ability to manifest itself. The true essence of Inspiration may have its maximum impact when we allow this energy to come to the self in the "spaces between our thoughts," and when we allow the ego to dissolve. (This notion of the ego will be discussed in detail in chapter twelve.)

At this point in our lives, we have developed a set of personal Beliefs and Philosophies. If we are unwavering in our convictions and unshakable in the faith we have established, we discover that we have become priests of something, rather than people who meander through life with no direction to their existence. These Beliefs and Philosophies give personal meaning, significance and individuality to the manner in which we walk through this life.

ten

Our Achievements

*I went to the woods because I wanted to
live deliberately, to suck the marrow from
the bones of life; to put to rout all that
was not life, and not to come to the end of
life, and discover that I had not lived.*
—HENRY DAVID THOREAU

It seems like so much of what we do in our lives pertains to our careers, defining who we are and how we present ourselves to society, and ultimately positioning our perceived place in the whole of humanity. I propose in this dimension of the human potential that we meditate on evaluating and understanding the true essence of who we are (the self). Once that is defined, we base our career, goals and achievements, and, ultimately, our life path on those meditated observations. Most important, we make a point to reflect on what the great love (passion) is in our life and how it can make its place in the world.

The planet Saturn is known for its karmic implication and is related to our careers, achievements, and business sense. It rules over the zodiac sign Capricorn. Karma, in this instance, refers to the seeds that we choose to plant with the express intent of creating a specific experience (in this chapter, it pertains to career), and the rewards we may reap if we nourish and nurture those seeds until our true desires become manifest. Karma, in all instances, has the same principle: what we sow, so shall we reap.

Saturn is the planet of karma *and* caution, so it is best that we proceed with the manifestation of our desires with a mindful gauge, carefully measuring and maintaining a sense of realistic expectations. Saturn can bring both rewards and repercussions in all the dimensions of the human potential. It would serve us well to remember and be mindful of all our actions knowing that the Lord of Karma will one day make us accountable for them. We may think no one is looking when we demonstrate our self as less than humanitarian, but alas, Saturn is always on the watch. The Lord of Karma does not rule with an iron fist, bidding humanity to carry out his deeds and administering punishment when he sees fit. This Lord is the true energy each individual emits from the self. What we radiate to the Universe will be returned to us; we are the Lords of our selves, which is contrary to what certain organized religions would have us believe.

The NBC television series *My Name is Earl* humorously portrays the basic principles of karma by bringing awareness of this theme to humanity in a lighthearted fashion. Understated suggestions of these cosmic realities were continually presented to humanity through the media as we progressed into the twenty-first century. And they continue to pop up all around us, as in the aforementioned *My Name is Earl*. Subtlety of message is required during this time of evolution so as not to overwhelm the population with its Karmic principles. Now planted in the fictional media garden, karma will slowly begin to grow, spreading itself into reality until its roots gain a strong foothold within humanity and subtle hints become a way of thinking about life. Hopefully, we are paying close attention.

The 1951 movie *The Day the Earth Stood Still* is another great example of how the Universe has used the media to insinuate subtle indicators into pop culture, signposts to alert humanity that it must be careful to steer its course away from self-obliteration. This message about the true nature of humanitarianism, which was ironically delivered by an alien culture, warned that unless humanity chose a path more in accord with the greater purpose for all, humanity would undoubtedly destroy itself. This film's premise is synonymous with the Universal way. The Universe does not interfere with the course of humanity, but rather suggests a better way, another path of co-existence, to humanity.

One theme in this film I find to be greatly profound is

that of equity and sharing of wealth and resources. During a conversation between Klaatu, the alien, and a young boy, Klaatu was astounded to learn that one human would not willingly share the wealth of his resources with another. This quite clearly illustrates the manner in which much of humanity behaves today, and has for many millennia. In this film, not only has humanity begun to destroy its own planet, but humanity's downfall will eventually radiate outward to other planets, as well, which is why Klaatu came to Earth. And so we discover another Universal message cloaked within this mainstream media product: we are all part of the intertwined cosmic connective of the All That Is.

THE MAGICAL LOVE OF CAREER

When we cross paths with someone who truly loves his career and is successful, we may find that the passion emerged from the individual himself while in the very process of building the career that gives him such joy. So what do we learn from this? Do what you desire and love above everything else and you will create your own opportunities to flourish in your career. Living in this state of being would surely change the way the workplace is perceived, for it would no longer be a place of work, but a place of delight–a place of light, filled with light!

One holiday season, I received a coffee mug as a gift from a dear friend; the words on it read, "Do what you like, like what you do: Life is good." I'm quite fond of that saying, but would change one thing about it. By substituting like with Love, we can add profound weight behind what it is we are choosing to accomplish in our worldly goals and achievements. There are many who pursue their chosen professions simply to earn the exorbitant salaries that some particular professions (medicine, law, finance, sports) may provide. But, if enjoyment of the job is not a reward of the career, then misery and discontentment will only ensue regardless of the size of the salary. The old adage is true: money can't buy happiness.

Thoreau once wrote: "Beware of all enterprises that require new clothes." Now I am not suggesting that certain careers, such as the ones I mentioned above, are strictly pursued out of greed. On the contrary. Many people become doctors to help heal the sick and to save lives. And stock brokers can aid families with saving for their future, such as for the children's education or the parents' retirement. But when the accumulation of wealth is the only motivation for pursuing a career, sadness and gloom will eventually befall the greedy person, then radiate out into humanity, affecting the lives of countless others.

I believe, as do many others, that if we choose what we do out of love for our careers, then grand amounts of abundance will certainly come to us; of course, we must also allow that abundance to return to us, as was discussed in chapter two. We must also ask ourselves, are we doing what we do for money or love? And I state, if we choose to do what we do for love, the money will easily follow.

If we were able to understand our true personal being and then strive toward creating a career that is congruent with that, the fulfillment and expression of this career process would be much more profound. There are those who can truly demonstrate this quality; however, the majority of humanity seems to meander through life bewildered about what to choose for a personal career path.

The career sector of the human potential seems to be the most definitive in regards to our Earthly achievements and the manner in which we demonstrate our being. So much of our everyday lives are consumed in an office environment. For some, it is in an office outside of their homes where they commute–for some individuals, that commute can add up to a ghastly amount of time–to a place that, for most individuals, is not a spiritual and highly evolved environment. And some create their office space in part of their everyday dwelling, their home. I, myself, make my office not far from my bedroom door, which, in and of itself, can present a challenge! It's easy to lose focus on your career when your home life is only feet away. And it's equally easy to let your home life fall by the wayside when your career is so tightly meshed in with your homelife.

Some may feel that doing something they truly love will not afford them the ability to simply survive in everyday life. Perhaps they feel they just do not have the skills and know-how to achieve those goals; they may not possess the contacts and connections, or perhaps they don't have something they feel is marketable and appealing. I know I've already referenced several writings by Thoreau so far, but I'd like to offer one more quote from this famous Transcendentalist that is apropos to this discussion.

> If one advances confidently in the direction of their dreams, and endeavors to lead a life which they have imagined, they will meet with a success unexpected in common hours.

The only abilities we need to possess in order to manifest those achievements is the desire, belief and diligence to make our dreams a reality. Once we are confident we can do so–then so shall it be!

The Magic will surely find us when we believe. I once received a greeting card that read, "Believe as a child believes and the magic will find you." It seems that as we progress into adulthood, the magic we once knew in childhood escapes us. This is not a quality that is "otherworldly" (or, for some, a quality of the underworld), but is simply the faith of existing in a place of knowingness so that all that is necessary for our existence will be provided to us in co-creation with the Universe. The magic that created the stars and the heavens and the Earth has been encoded within the wiring of our being. A long time ago, Stevie Nicks mused, "Don't you know that the stars are part of us." The magic will make itself known to us once we believe that we have that ability within ourselves.

WHATEVER YOUR HEART DESIRES

Desire is a great thing. It is the conscious fuel that stokes the fire within us so that we may continually advance toward the creation and achievement of anything in our lives. Desire comes from inspiration, which we discussed in the prior chapter, that fuels our creative forces and does not come from desirous or covetous feelings for material things. It is the impetus to create that propels us to do whatever it is that we choose to do. Desire is the catalyst for the development and manifestation of our dreams, goals, achievements, and visions of the creation of our futures.

Desire will allow us to continue the process of creation, growth and development with any given idea. We simply need to nurture these desires upon a strong and stable Foundation, as we discussed in chapter four. And this is the polar balance of that discussion since we are now building upon that Foundation. With nourishment and patience, we can begin to see those desires manifest into something real and tangible.

FOLLOW THE LEADER

There are moments in our lives when it may be necessary to become a leader. This is the opposite of the nurturer role model discussed in chapter four. This is what one may perceive as the authority figure and/or the disciplinarian, and it pertains to both leadership of the self and leadership of others. Here, authority is not defined as one who has power over another; it is one who has the ability to guide others through the creation of their desires in order to achieve their goals.

This authority figure, regardless of who it may be in physical form (mother, father, boss, mentor, etc.), will assist in our stability and create a condition of check and balance in our lives so that we remain grounded once we secure our achievements. There may be those moments when, in order for us to carry out the creation of our goals and to strive toward our achievements, we need to call upon the assistance of others. When we create our goals and accomplishments at the highest level of existence, we will gladly choose to share the wealth with those who have assisted us in manifesting those achievements.

This leader/authority figure is necessary in the process of realizing this aspect of our potential, as it gives us the required boundaries that assist us in remaining appropriately realistic and cautious (two very distinct qualities of our Karmic friend Saturn) when manifesting our achievements in dicey situations.

WHY AM I HERE?

Many of us roam through this life bewildered, continuously analyzing and reevaluating the grand purpose for the self in this life. We question why the Universe sent us to this Earth, as if there is some old man with a beard up in the sky who has a plan for our life, but is, instead, playing some great cosmic chess game with us as the pawns. We stand there without knowledge about or input into what will become of us until that Lord of fate moves us on the chess board, thus creating our purpose for us. I suggest that our purpose is whatever we choose it to be. Simple? Yes. I also suggest that one's purpose may also include the very process of discovering one's *raison d'être*–as the French would say–our reason for being.

Perhaps the process of discovery is what that individual being has come to Earth to experience. Through the process of wonder and discovery, the individual discovers herself as a creative being, which is the truth of what she has been designed to uncover. This process of discovery can also be of great significance once she has realized her chosen path, as it gives her an appreciation for the trials and tribulations that have played an intricate role in the manifestation of these understandings.

WHY AM I *REALLY* HERE?

I have come to know and understand that our reason for coming to this planet–that reason might be different if we were born on Venus or Mars or another planet in this vast Galaxy, but for the matters of this discussion we use Earth as our point of reference–is to experience our selves as the creative beings we have designed. Just as the Greatness and the Allness created the Heavens and the Earth, so, too, do we create our reality with the intention of experiencing the reality we have created, along with the outcomes of that creation and its interaction with all of humanity. Anyone who blames another being or outside forces for the condition of his life has no concept of the power of creation that is instilled within him.

As I stated in chapter three, if we were to pay attention to our every thought throughout our existence, we would, over time, come to know exactly how we created the conditions of our lives and the reality that surrounds us. I will add that this is not limited to our present incarnation, for, in the moments of the grand infinite, this is something that we carry within the essence of the self, from previous incarnations into this life and through to the next. The process of creation is everlasting and ubiquitous.

DESTINY VS. FATE

To understand destiny requires us to accept as fact that as we move through this experience called life, every day we are creating, re-creating and co-creating with the Universe the potential within ourselves with awareness and with purpose. Destiny is ever changing, ever progressing, forever evolving. The concept of fate suggests we have no choice in or control of the conditions of our life and that our experience here is written in stone. Destiny, on the other hand, is the continuation of the process of creation and evolution–the evolution of the essence of that which we truly are and what we are determined to become, which is also the essence of what we truly are. Our destiny will manifest itself from awareness; fate will come to pass out of unconsciousness and the absence of awareness of the self.

So, what is it we are striving to become? I would pose that it is whatever we would choose to become while we are embodied in this human form. Let me repeat: we have come to this Earthly inhabitation to experience the process of creating with the power of the mind. It is purely up to the individual, hand in hand with free will, as to how these Earthly incarnations will manifest.

GOALS AND GROWTH

The creation and the manifestation of our goals help us to progress to and through various stages in our lives and carry us to the next station. The process of creating our goals and the execution and achievement of those goals provide fulfillment and joy. They may act as measuring points for where we've been, as well as assist in the creative process as we choose where to direct the course of our lives. We establish our goals according to our desires and what it is we choose to create and experience.

Goals are an integral part of our growth process; without them we remain stagnant, as it is necessary for the self and the spirit to have this experience of fulfillment and joy. Without them, we feel empty and void. The sense of accomplishment we experience once we have achieved a goal provides us with a sense of fulfillment and demonstrates our creative potential.

When we reflect upon the path traveled, the goals and achievements provide a gauge to measure the accomplishments over a given period of time. Though the magnitude of some goals may be greater, the sense of fulfillment and accomplishment never diminishes whether we choose to beat the odds of a life-threatening illness, climb to the top of the Himalayas, write a book, or simply create a day filled with peace and harmony. The Universe will acknowledge all things as equal, regardless of the magnitude. As scribed by Dr. Helen Schucman in *A Course of Miracles*, "There is no order of difficulty in Miracles. One is not harder or bigger than another. They are all the same. All expressions of Love are maximal." Perhaps we can take a hint from this passage and choose that all our goals and achievements while we reside on this Earthly dimension of consciousness–and into the next dimension–become expressions of maximal Love.

Goals provide the self with a means of opportunity to reach beyond seeming limitations. The creation of a project of grand proportion may seem daunting, but when the smaller goals are established as stepping stones on the path to the creation of something larger, the task at hand does not seem as difficult. The smaller goals are the building blocks in the foundation of a considerably greater goal.

SERVICE

> Everybody can be great...because anybody
> can serve. You don't have to have a college
> degree to serve. You don't have to make your
> subject and verb agree to serve. You only
> need to have a heart full of grace. A soul gen-
> erated by love.

Martin Luther King, Jr. said that about an individual's
ability to serve his fellow man. The ideology of service is
characterized by how, through our personal efforts and
achievements, we choose to contribute to humanity and
how this individual contribution to the greater good of
humanity dictates how we fit into the whole of humanity. If we are only self-serving–without balance–then what
are we really doing for humanity? We may define service
as being a part of and contributing to the benefit and creation of the greater whole. Looking to serve oneself alone
is not being of service, for one who seeks to only serve
the self has little awareness of the greater connection to
the wholeness of humanity and the All That Is.

It is true that we need to earn an income so that we
have a means for survival, which includes paying the
mortgage, buying groceries, and even, at times, enjoying
a bit of luxury and entertainment. As we discussed in
chapter two, abundance is intended for every individual,
so I suggest that whatever it is we choose to do while we
are in this human form as it relates to our career, let the
creation of this aspect of our human potential be something that will be of service–contributing to the greater

part of the whole–to humanity. We create this service as something that contributes, benefits, influences, inspires, and stimulates the greater existence of humanity.

If one chooses to be an educator, let that one educate in a manner that is unbiased and free of prejudice, regardless of the educator's individual convictions, so that the full scope of all subjects can be presented to the pupil. If one chooses to be a housekeeper, let that one go into every home and bless the environment and fill it with radiant light. Regardless of what the action may be, let the intention that envelopes the action be filled with love, peace, and harmony so that each and every action, no matter how seemingly small, will be of greater service to humanity. As Albert Schweitzer once said: "I don't know what your destiny will be, but one thing I know: the only ones among you who will be really happy are those who will have sought and found how to serve."

DON'T FEAR THE REAPER: KARMA!

Whatever it is that we radiate out to the Universe will be returned to the self; this is Saturn's great reminder. Saturn defines how we must be accountable for not only our actions, regardless of what they are, but also the intentions behind those actions, for that is where Saturn is certain to render us accountable.

When we are aware of the principles of karma in this dimension of the human potential, we find ourselves thinking twice about the intentions behind our actions, especially when we choose to embark upon a particular career path. If we take conscious action in our business dealings that are less than honest with our affiliates, that lack of honesty will be returned to us in some form or another. If we steal something from another, regardless of the quantity or value, in some manner, we will be held accountable by the Universe for that action. The laws created by humanity may not always catch us, but the laws of the Universe will see to it that we are held responsible.

KARMA GOES ROUND IN CIRCLES

A great deal of the composition of our achievements stems from what we call karma; what we put out into the Universe will return to us. Karma is the eminent gift from Saturn, the large planetary body in our solar system that keeps us in check and balance–Saturn is exalted and dignified by his occupation in the realm of balance and it's where he finds he is of greatest service. Just as nature maintains a balance in all things, Saturn makes certain that the Universal laws are clearly exposed and then enforces that balance through karma.

Saturn creates his home in Capricorn, the sign of goals and achievements. Capricorn strives to influence beings to reach for the greatest potential of the self. It is through the execution and accomplishment of the goals and achievements that we uncover the power of creation encoded in each individual. With the manifestation of these goals and achievements, we can reflect upon and appreciate the progress we have achieved along the path of humanity.

The desires, which are born from inspiration, are cultivated into a personal drive to serve for the benefit and evolution of humanity. When we are one with all humanity and conscious of that truth, we can strive to become something greater than ourselves in our careers and the achievements that manifest themselves out of the desire for growth on a personal and global scale. Through this process, we not only enter into service for the benefit of humanity but we enter into service to become one with the essence of the true self.

eleven

Awareness

On a group of theories one can found a school; but on a group of values one can found a culture, a civilisation, a new way of living together among men.
—IGNAZIO SILONE

As we progress toward this next dimension of the human potential–Awareness–we have come to understand a higher level of consciousness about the realities we have created. At this point, we can delve deeper into the broad scope of that consciousness that now advances to Awareness. In the astrological realm, the planet that is associated with Awareness is Uranus, whose home sign is Aquarius.

From the great chaos that was the beginning of the formation of our solar system emerged symmetry and perfection. So, too, in our own lives, can awareness emerge from chaos, which the God of Chaos (Uranus) will create. In this instance, chaos refers not to a state of mass confusion and pandemonium where rhyme and reason do not exist, but rather as it is illustrated in Edward Lorenz's early 1960s Chaos Theory:

> [Chaos] refers to an apparent lack of order in a system that nevertheless obeys particular laws or rules; this understanding of chaos is synonymous with dynamical instability, a condition discovered by the physicist Henri Poincare in the early 20th century.

Underlying what seems to be a state of mayhem and disorder, there exists a symmetry and perfection in chaos when it is allowed to unfold, as it did with the creation of our solar system. This conglomeration of bedlam will regain the consciousness of perfection from its perfection, for it has been and is being created by the All That Is. Before our solar system remembered its perfection, it existed as a mass, a clump of clutter—a condition that can exist in Human life. Once it began to remember the perfection of itself, all things fell into place. The planets formed and took their position around the sun. And the moons and comets and asteroids did the same. This, too, is demonstrated in our existence when we remember our perfection. And just as all the objects in our solar system continue to move toward their perfect state, so do we strive for the same.

This process is something we do in our own everyday humanness. In the aftermath of what seems to be a condition of chaos, do we not experience the condition of an awakening or, in psychoanalytical terms, a breakthrough? This is in part the significance of the planet Uranus; out of what seems to be chaos will arise a great awakening that is embraced by Awareness.

As is now evident with the condition of our planet, it seems as though the media daily bombards humanity with images of chaos. The transit of Uranus through the sign of Pisces from late 2003 through March 20, 2011, is awakening that which resides deep within the unconsciousness of humanity. The Great Awakener (Uranus) is, in astrological terms, in mutual reception to Neptune, the planet of the subconscious and the undoing of one's self. Neptune is also transiting the sign of Awakenings, Aquarius. These two gigantic heavenly bodies are traveling through the signs of the zodiac in which the other rules.

I perceive these Universal messages to indicate that humanity has arrived at a time in history when it will uncover aspects of itself that have been buried deep within the unconscious. Though humanity is currently existing with a lack of awareness, by going through this process of chaos we are presently enduring on Earth, humanity will usher in the opportunity to experience itself as a spiritual being housed in human form. I urge that this is an opportunity that we should not ignore. Whatever the outcome, humanity will make a choice in the coming years that will dictate how the ensuing millennia will unfold.

If that Awareness is to be revealed to humanity's greater collective self, we must allow change to take place, both as individuals and as a people. (Uranus is also the God of Great Change.) We may experience at various times in our lives moments that seem to be riddled with bedlam–then it all seems to fall effortlessly into place...sometimes. From the chaos can arise an Awareness of the self, and from that Awareness we can create an existence radiant with perfect love, peace, trust, symmetry, and harmony. Aren't these the qualities of existence that most individuals desire? And not to repeat myself, but if we are to choose those qualities within ourselves and in the world, we must allow and experience change to unfold.

Gandhi once said: "You must be the change you wish to see in the world." When change is permitted within the self, this condition will radiate and manifest itself out to the world. When we operate with Awareness, we are no longer unaware of our place in humanity and the intricate, interwoven, synergistic dynamic we entwine with humanity; we finally grasp that we are all one. If the condition of our planet is to change, the change must take place first within the self. If we are to choose the expression of world peace, we must experience the condition of peace within the self first and foremost. The world is in its present condition as a result of the collective unconsciousness of humanity.

This is the Dawning...

The impending Age of Aquarius is almost upon us. The precise year has been debated for centuries, though many astrologers and New Age experts put the date circa 2135. However, all but few spiritualists agree that the Age of Aquarius ushers in a time of raised levels of consciousness, Awareness, and the true understanding of the oneness of humanity. Hopefully, this will all come to pass. I say hopefully because, again, as with all things, we are at choice as to how we will give life to the energies of the potential planetary phenomena in the years to come. We may again know an era like the ancient civilizations of Atlantis and Lemuria experienced. Perhaps this time humanity will not obliterate itself when technology far outreaches humanity's ability to usefully apply its capabilities. This is something that will come to pass over many decades, not something we will surprisingly awaken to one morning.

In the 1960s, we sang that it was the "the dawning of the Age of Aquarius." I would suggest something more accurate: that period may have been the birth of the beginning before the dawning of the Age of Aquarius. Let me explain.

The outer planets in our solar system–Uranus, Neptune, and Pluto–are known as the generational planets; they have influence over an entire generation more so than on a personal level. Yes, these outer planets do have importance in the individual horoscope; however, the relationships between those outer planets at a given moment can and will describe the potential of the given generation born at that time.

The significant planetary configurations of the 1960s–especially during the mid-60s–deal with the planets Neptune and, our humanitarian friend, Uranus, as well as our Dark Knight, Pluto. Both Uranus and Pluto traveled through the sign of Virgo virtually at the same point in the sky during the mid-1960s. Neptune was approximately 60 degrees away from both those planets in the sign of Scorpio. This degree of separation between these distant and massive heavenly bodies presents one of humanity's opportunities to gain awareness of its more highly evolved potential that it inhabits as we progress into this cosmic age.

This is the generation, I feel, that is to usher in the true New Age/Age of Aquarius, especially now as these energies of those planetary configurations are activated. As I have stated, this time of profound change and transformation was born during the 1960s because the children born unto that time are those who will also carry us into the age of consciousness and awareness of the human potential.

Consciousness Vs. Awareness

Some may suggest that consciousness and awareness are one and the same–I suggest otherwise. So how is the beginning of Awareness different from the beginnings of consciousness? Conscious reality deals with the under-standing of our thoughts and how they create and affect our personal reality. Awareness is the understanding of that consciousness and how it fits into the whole of humanity–it's the clarity of the bigger picture.

In the painting *Sunday Afternoon on the Island of la Grande Jatte* by the neo-impressionist George Seurat, when the spectator views the painting at close range, all that is observed are tiny dots of color–the spectator can see only the tiny particles of something of larger scale. But as we move farther away from the image, we see a joining of those particles to form a whole–we can see the bigger picture. This is a fitting example of how consciousness can be the dots and how Awareness is the collection of all those dots seen from afar that make up that painting.

Another example would be an observer standing on the top of a skyscraper looking down upon the sidewalk. He will view individual people as specks moving along the streets. He might see trees swaying to and fro in the breeze. And maybe the ebb and flow of the river water against the shoreline. If we then move farther away out into space, we would see the entire Earth as a whole, liv-ing organism and not as those individual specks on the sidewalks and the trees and water. This is the depiction that needs to be kept in mind: the notion of humanity as a particle of this whole and living organism. We are not separate from that oneness of nature's majesty.

Awareness is the first stage in the process of Knowing,

which we will review in the final chapter of this discussion of the human potential. Awareness can be seen as the understanding of how one's reality fits into the greater whole of humanity, and on the grander scale, the Universe. We come to understand that we are not separate from each other, but that we are truly one.

All the actions of mankind can and will have some sort of effect on the collective group of the planet. So when one terrorist embarks upon a suicide mission and kills hundreds, that one individual is not only affecting the families of those victims, but the extended family of the population of this Earth. Other examples of more profound impact were the attacks on New York City and Washington, D.C., on September 11, 2001. On that dark day, was not each and every member of humanity touched in some way by the horrific acts and moved by compassion for each of the victims' families?

Those unfathomable events alerted humanity to the horrors that it can inflict upon itself from the condition of a lack of awareness. On that somber day, did it not appear as though the Earth stood still? Regardless of one's physical location on the planet on that day, no one of this human race was left untouched by those events. This is not to lessen the pain and sorrow caused to those families and friends of the loved ones who perished on that day, but to acknowledge the interconnectedness of each individual regardless of one's race, creed, color, or sexual orientation. In the period leading up to those events, humanity was observing the process of manifesting tragedy that humanity can create upon itself. The end result is that humanity may come to know itself as a spiritual being within a human form and realize its creative force and presence in and with the Universe.

If we, as humanity, choose to move forward aware of our connection with each other, we will not again experience the events that unfolded on September 11, 2001. I say these words with great affirmation; the choice will always be ours. Not the workings of some great Deity in the Heavens or some demon from the depths of Hell, but out of the choices made by the human condition when it becomes aware of itself as a facet of the All That Is, which through the greatness of its resourcefulness created the Heavens and the Earth and all the stars and planets, galaxies, quasars and nebulae. This same illustrious power is within the fiber of each human being; the time is at hand for the awareness of this greatness.

Ultimate Reality

What truly is real? Our reality on this Earthly dimension is directly related to our experiences while we exist on the Earth plane. We measure the passage of time against the events in our lives as they occur on any given day, and there are also those moments in history when we measure an entire lifetime against one event.

The majority of humanity uses a timepiece to measure the progression of the events, which correlates to the passage of the Sun across the skies during what we refer to as a day. But for that Sun, what is the passage of a day? It has no point of reference or measure of relativity as we would understand it other than its children, the planets. Certainly, if one were to stand on the Sun and look up to the Heavens, the planets will appear to rise and set; but, what is the measure of "time" during which that rising and setting will correspond? Perhaps being out in space would give us a glimpse of something known as ultimate reality or that which is absolute. Ultimate reality, quite simply, just "is." We would observe while out in space that one planetary body exists in its relativity to another.

The similarity of this relativity while on earth could be analogous to the directions of left and right and up and down. When one person is facing another, an object to one's right is, in reality, to the left of the other. When we look up to that airplane flying in the sky, the passengers are looking down upon us. The passengers are up in the sky to the observer on the ground, but an astronaut in orbit would look down upon those same airplane passengers. Once again, this is not indicative of something being wrong or right, but how one thing is different to two individuals respective to their relative perspective. Human reality is dependant upon the individual's place on the Earth and in the grand scheme of the All That Is, his position and place along the evolutionary scale.

While we are in the physical form, we can attempt to

understand this concept, but not until we move through to a higher level of consciousness can we further grasp the wholeness of this notion. In a way, we are not meant to completely understand this, or we may not want to continue our existence on Earth. As we progress to a greater level of Awareness, we can begin to understand that the knowingness of all that we experience while on this plane is relative to our personal experience. Perhaps, with this knowingness, we may become respectful of others and their own personal experiences.

While we are having this Earthly experience we are accountable only for our personal behaviors and actions–in other words, we are not our brother's keeper. This is not to say we should disconnect from one another, but rather that we must be respectful of another's process of evolution even in those moments when we may feel it imperative to "help" another by imposing our will. One's process of evolution may not be clear to a second individual as they each experience this world of the relative; but with Awareness, the second can understand that the growth and evolution of the first, in its individuality, in some way is making its own unique contribution to the development, creation, and evolution of humanity.

For even in those horrific experiences of war and destruction, as demonstrated on September 11, the hope would be that through those experiences, we, as humanity, are coming to know ourselves as the creative beings we have designed. May we choose to progress to a new level of understanding about the connection we all have in our humanness and timelessness, and then make choices that would be conducive to the progress of humanity. Regardless of how we perceive each other, in reality, we all have ten fingers and toes, two eyes and ears, one mouth and nose. Are we really that different from one another regardless of race, creed, sexual orientation or color?

This is also not so say that we consciously allow some individuals to inflict abuse upon other individuals. If we find that we have created such a situation, we may reflect upon those conditions that brought that particular experience to the realm of our reality and then make adjustments to those behaviors and conditions that manifested the said situation. Ultimately, the end result is that we stop creating abusive and destructive experiences.

SOCIAL CIRCLES

When choosing our social circle, it would seem that we select our friends on a conscious level and our family on an unconscious level. Ultimately, we're all part of the same Universe, regardless of the biological connection. The social sphere of reality allows us to go beyond the immediate family, granting the opportunity to extend our circle to non-familial relations, thus expanding our Awareness of the reality of the self. In a way, we are extending our sphere of reality with the Awareness of our global community. This is another aspect of the multifaceted dimension of Awareness, which extends beyond our homes, outside into the world, encircling and encompassing the planet we inhabit.

The dynamics of the relationships that come to pass among the biological family and our extended family of friends is something that transcends from lifetime to lifetime. These connections are our tribe. Native Americans have a great understanding of this quality. Individual spirits have an intricate influence on each other that gets carried from one lifetime to another. These etheric bonds are never really broken, for they are part of the continuum of the All That Is.

Through the interaction of these social experiences, we may encounter our first understandings of how our personal realities coexist with others in the global community. The interaction among friends and the dynamic exchange of camaraderie allows one the opportunity to experience the self in relation to another. From the understanding of this one-on-one relationship, we then move to the higher understanding of the social experience with many individuals that ripples out to greater communities, then to those faraway places. Ultimately, we understand that we are all a part of the greatness of the whole.

LOVE RECEIVED

Oftentimes, the notion of "it's better to give than to receive" manipulates and defines the manner in which love returns to us. We must choose to allow love to come back to us in our lives if we are to experience love. Receiving love is meaningful in maintaining a state of "in-balance," and not imbalance. We would serve one another well by not only giving love, but also in receiving it. The dynamic exchange of giving and receiving love, regardless of whether or not the relationship is of a platonic nature, must be something that is constant in order for one to experience the fullness of the exchange.

When we allow ourselves to feel the love from our comrades on a conscious level, we have the opportunity to experience the dynamic quality of the relationship more deeply and profoundly. If we only give and do not allow ourselves to receive, we may close ourselves off to others and create an incomplete sense of oneness.

In terms of receiving Love on the humanitarian dimension, we would be served well to remember that the love we give to humanity will be returned to us, as well. We can begin this process by demonstrating a love and respect of nature, for Earth, nature's great creation, is our first home.

Moving Toward Humanitarianism

When we experience the epiphany of finding ourselves existing in a manner that is humanitarian, we also realize how we are a component of the greater whole of humanity. Here we have the true essence of the beginning of awareness. We come to an understanding that everything we do will ripple out and have a continuous effect on others.

As I have discussed, the chaos of the formation of our solar system manifested the symmetry and perfection of our planetary dynasty. The Chaos Theory suggests that though there seems to be a state of confusion, there is an underlying confidence, order, and understanding: the Laws of the Universe. These are laws not created by the human condition, but by matters of the energy exchange that exist regardless of the awareness of these states of affairs. These Universal Laws simply exist whether we are conscious of them or not. However, I tell you this: We, as a people, are approaching a time when we will become acutely aware of the great majesty and power of these Universal Laws.

There are seven Universal Laws and for those who are interested in learning more about these principles, I would suggest reading Deepak Chopra's *The Seven Spiritual Laws of Success*. Earlier, I referred to the law of "Cause and Effect," which simply states "what goes around comes around." What we put out to the Universe will be returned to us, and as I mentioned in chapter ten, Saturn will make certain of that.

There is also something known as The Butterfly Effect. This is an extension of Edward Lorenz's interpretation of Chaos Theory that was mentioned earlier in this chapter. By the 1970s, Lorenz had refined this Butterfly Effect concept conceived by an unnamed meteorologist into a paper that he titled *Predictability:*

Does the Flap of a Butterfly's Wings in Brazil Set off a Tornado in Texas? I think the title says it all and needs no further explanation (though it's an intriguing concept to research). Every action we take has a ripple effect on the world around us.

This example of the flap of a butterfly's wings may be somewhat extreme, but let's look at the theory from a different perspective. On a smaller scale, fill a container with water and stir it quickly with a spoon. Once the water is spinning sufficiently, stop stirring the spoon but continue to hold it in the water. The spoon and the water haven't physically changed, but the change in movement by the spoon begins to affect the movement of the water.

We, as individuals, are greater when we're living a part of something greater (i.e., humanity) than when we exist only for ourselves. In other words, the sum of the parts is greater than the whole. Whether or not we are conscious how each and every thought, word, and action created by an individual may affect one individual or all of humanity, all that we do, in fact, does have consequences. Humanity, in its somewhat limited vision, is not always aware that this truth can be reality. Once we move into the condition of Awareness, this is when the shift can begin.

Through Awareness, Billions Become One

In this section, we have reviewed how our own individual existence on this planet is essentially a part of the greater whole of humanity and the All That Is. As we become aware that humanity is spirit vibration in human form, we also begin to notice that for every action, there can and will be an equal and opposite reaction. Just like when we cast a rock into a pond and observe the water ripple to the outer most regions of that pond, so, too, do our actions ripple out into humanity during our existence on this Earth.

The planet Uranus, also known as "The Great Awakener," will elevate us to higher levels of awareness of the self; how the self affects and creates the reality of humanity on the global scale is partly due to his counterpart Aquarius, the zodiac representation of humanitarianism. Through Awareness, we can begin to understand the connections of the Global Village, that we are part of one community–the wholeness of humanity–and even in our actions we are not separate from one another.

Uranus will create a condition of chaos in the individual life and in the self that is the whole of humanity so that the individual and humanity can experience Awareness through the conditions that are created. Whenever we are faced with a condition of chaos–not chaos as a condition of dysfunctional disarray, but as a divine order attempting to come together in a way that will serve a greater purpose–the self and humanity are presented with the opportunity to experience themselves as being greater than themselves, as was the order that created our planetary home out of the spinning chaos of matter and Spirit.

twelve

Knowing

The source of all creation is pure consciousness...pure potentiality seeking expression from the unmanifest to the manifest. And when we realize that our true Self is one of pure potentiality, we align with the power that manifests everything in the universe.
—DEEPAK CHOPRA

As we embark upon this last dimension of the human potential, we begin to understand ourselves dwelling in this human form as ethereal beings occupying a physical body in order to experience the human condition as creative beings. May we return to a state of remembrance of how we are all one from the same source, and how we have returned to this Earth so that we may come to know and experience ourselves as the creative beings that we have been designed to be.

This potential of creating the reality in which we live has been encoded in each and every living form. It empowers the same creative potential and dynamics as the all-encompassing All That Is, which created this Earthly place and the Heavens and the Universe. When we have come to know and understand this potential that resides within the fiber of every being, we progress to a place of simply knowing that we are all part of that same whole, which is the All That Is.

Humanity has now arrived at a time when it has progressed beyond the need to know itself simply as part of this whole–the collective we–who inhabit the Earth. We must progress to an understanding that we are a particle of something much greater that extends beyond our Earthly home. We are part of the Universe and whatever may exist beyond its farthest limits.

I now state this as I write these words in this last chapter of my great journal (April 14, 2006, 10:14 a.m., EDT): it is a necessity that the greater whole of humanity progresses to this condition of Knowing and understanding itself as the greater part of the All That Is, and in that greatness, we are not separate from one another regardless of our location in the Universe. Our individualistic way of thinking has never served a greater purpose for humanity.

Events will come to pass on this Earth that will strongly suggest Humanity must choose to know itself as part of this greater whole and that separation is a mindset of something primitive, regardless of the color of one's skin or geographical location on Earth. Unless this understanding and condition of Knowing is welcomed into the individual self, humanity will experience events that will dwarf the incidents of September 11, 2001, and earlier events such as the Holocaust and the atomic bombings of Hiroshima and Nagasaki.

I say these words not to instill fear in the hearts of humanity, for many religions have done a good job of that on their own. I have been given this vision in the hope that all members of humanity will make the choice to realize the magnificent, unique, and individual potential that lies within themselves and that we may choose to find a better way in the hopes of creating a world of peace, harmony, and unity, Knowing we are all one.

In order for the understanding of this principle to make itself known to humanity, there is potential that an event will come to pass that may not be of this Earth. Let me explain.

On September 11, 2001, those from foreign lands attacked the United States. It was simple to see who the enemy was in this instance. Though was is really? The United Stated embarked upon its "War on Terror"; insurgency ran rampant in Iraq; thousands upon thousands of men and women, regardless of on which side of the dividing line they stood, surrendered their lives in the pursuit of "freedom." I am still not convinced the war in Iraq has served a greater purpose, but that is another discussion for another book.

The possibility of which I am speaking in this instance could be some crisis that does not originate of this Earth, but rather one from, perhaps...space.

Scientists have speculated that during the 2011 time-frame, there will be significant solar flare and storm activity. There has also been much talk among New Age spiritualists and philosophers about a time greatly anticipated, particularly 2011–and this is no accident, as, astrologically, the time between 2010-2012 will signify a momentous era on the planet in terms of humanity's awareness of its possibilities and potentials. At the time of this writing in 2006, solar flares have been relatively quiet; they seem to be nonexistent or, more accurately, they are dormant and have simply completed a cycle. (All things in the Universe are cyclical.)

The cycle will begin again, and the next cycle will be much stronger than then previous one, according to information on NASA's website. During the time of 2011, the activity of solar flares has great potential to reach the highest level in recorded time. There was a period in 1958 that produced a high level of solar activity; however, the impending solar event has potential to be 30-50% stronger.*

The result of the energy burst emitted from the intensity of these solar flares has the potential, upon reaching the Earth, to create a global blackout. Again, I state this is potential and not something set in stone. Even before the full impact of this storm reaches us, we will begin to experience its effects. As it intensifies, the world will

*NASA: http://www.nasa.gov/vision/universe/solarsystem/10mar_stormwarning.html

experience difficulty with communications, cell phones, computers, and, perhaps, automobiles. Ultimately, the effects of the solar flares will result in a global blackout as transformers and power plants around the world are rendered powerless from the intense and explosive electromagnetic surges.

If these solar storms are on an eleven-year cycle, why will this impending storm affect us so differently than in the past? Simple. At no other time in history has humanity been so reliant on electrical power. In the last fifty years, humanity has created a pervasive trust in its electrical conveniences. Practically everything we use relies on electricity, whether from a socket in the wall or a battery. And our communications are dependant upon the satellites orbiting the Earth. In previous minor solar storms, some disruption was experienced and even a few satellites stopped working. Now imagine what would happen in a greater storm. Who knows the outcome when these things just randomly shut down for an unknown length of time.

Solar flares also can affect weather systems. Imagine the resulting weather from solar storms of this predicted magnitude.

This would be a crisis not created as the direct result of humanity's hand, but rather something of origin greater than humanity itself, though humanity would have had a hand in setting the stage. If an event or crisis of this magnitude were to occur, who would we retaliate against? The Sun? This event would present an opportunity for humanity to come together, regardless of who they are, and view each other as related, connected, as mothers and fathers, brothers and sisters, sons and daughters. This isn't meant in the blood relative sense, but rather in the sense that we are all part of the extended family that is humankind.

George Bernard Shaw once wrote: "The worst sin toward our fellow creatures is not to hate them, but to be indifferent to them; that's the essence of inhumanity." We sometimes view others to whom we have no physical connection (like those connections we have with family, friends, co-workers) as just objects without meaning to us. And this is where humanity can fail each other.

The late José Silva taught this profound philosophy to his students. If humanity would see each other as truly interconnected with each other, we might think twice about what we do to each another. Unfortunately, it may take a catastrophic event of worldwide proportions for humanity to comprehend and appreciate this power.

The potential intensity of the solar flares at this time, as opposed to another point in time, is a result of the planetary configurations at this particular period in the history of the Universe. The surge of energy, which I discussed in earlier chapters, is presenting humanity with several opportunities. First, for humanity to know itself as something greater than it believes itself to be. Second, that humanity has the potential to alter the course of events through the understanding of itself and the power and potential that lies within each and every being. Third, that humanity as individuals must come to know themselves to be one, rather than separate, in the All That Is and that the greatness of the creative power instilled within each human's being is as powerful on its own as it is as a part of the whole.

The Earth is NOT doomed for destruction; we have the power to alter the direction of energies, if we so choose. It is that simple, for we have made this process much more complicated than necessary.

In 1999, everyone around the world prepared together for the imminent Y2K problem, in which computer programs and operating systems were not programmed to recognize the change from 1999 to 2000. There were some who prophesied the end of the world as we knew it, that all computers would cease functioning. Planes would fall from the sky. Power plants would shut down. This solar flare problem is similar, though on a much greater scale and brought on by a force over which we have no control. But we can still prepare together, one humanity securing the world against the storms.

When we see all things as being of a single energy foundation from which we are all created, we then have the potential to alter and redirect how that energy becomes manifest. As Mr. Albert Einstein eloquently explained: "Energy can not be created or destroyed, only transformed." We have the ability to transform the course of this energy through the positive power of the mind, as well as the potential of the etheric being.

I will discuss in greater detail the possibilities and potential of future events in my next book, tentatively titled *Prophecies and Potentials: 2010-2012*.

COME INTO THE AWARENESS

Through Awareness, the knowing of the true self shall rise above the illusion of the human condition. The physical form of the human being is like a costume that the Spirit wears while experiencing this human understanding. When this brilliant disguise is no longer of use to the spirit, the truth of the self becomes known once again. This mask is what is known as the ego, or the fog of illusion created by Neptune, which has influence over this aspect of the human potential. We will come to understand that once this fog has been lifted, the essence of spirituality will encompass our etheric being.

The ego is what gets in the way of the true self as it experiences its human interaction. In psychological studies, it is defined as the conscious self. From my metaphysical perspective, the ego is the accumulation of the conditions we place upon the self, defining who it is we think we should be or what it is we think we should be doing: all aspects of the conscious self. The ego thinks it is better than the true self, so there is a constant battle for one to become dominant over the other. The ego is composed of these external factors that are half-truths of the wholeness of the true spiritual being.

The fog that Neptune creates is the ego, which masks the true essence of the self. Once the ego has been dissolved, we have the ability to view the self and the external world with crystal clarity at the highest sense of spirituality. This clarity will come to pass once we drop the ego–get out of our own way–and allow the true essence of divinity to inspire the highest creative aspect of the self.

This is that dimension of the human potential that can be the most abstract and elusive, as all things Neptunian may seem to be. In this instance, we are not dealing with what comes from the physical world, but from that which is ethereal, which is, in truth, the bona fide essence of who we are and the ever-present and indissoluble connection to the oneness of the All That Is. In this case, we have the influence of Neptune, the planet of higher knowing, spirituality and our higher spiritual powers, spiritual love, and illusion and euphoria. Pisces, the sign of the zodiac ruled by Neptune, also has these connotations.

USE THE FORCE

In the 1977 blockbuster *Star Wars*, George Lucas offered a very powerful message about trusting the instinct. A significant lesson young Luke Skywalker needed to learn was to "trust the force." I see this as a metaphor of humanity's need to remember to "know" itself and the trust we must have for the higher self. All that we truly need to know and understand is already encoded within the fabric of our being–we just need to go within ourselves to rediscover and remember that part of the greater self. When we remember, we unite with the member–we come together with that part of the self–that we already are. This is the highest level of our being.

One might ponder why we have come to this Earth without the tools needed to exist in harmony devoid of suffering and pain. However, one must also realize that both pain and suffering do have their place, so their consequences are not in vain. If it were not for those virtues, we would lack appreciation for the process of the journey. I am suggesting the knowingness will pave a much smoother path for the journey.

Trusting intuition and existing in a highly evolved state of being can lead us to a place of peace, harmony, and euphoria. We can even view this as an equation: peace plus harmony equals euphoria–not euphoria in the sense of escapism, but as the essence of the true nature that we would call Heaven. On the planetary level, Venus represents peace and harmony, the higher octave of that heavenly body is Neptune, the planet of euphoria. Again, euphoria, in the context of this material, is what some might call Heaven, or others might call a heavenly existence.

When those who have had a near-death event describe it, they often say the experience is like being in a euphoric state, some place that is of great peace, harmony, and tranquility that is not of this Earthly place. Through the knowingness within, we may understand this state of being, yet not fully comprehend its profundity, for if we were to possess a complete Knowing of that state, certainly we would not want to continue in human form, thus illuminating the reason for our forgetfulness of that place known as Heaven.

So much of what we seem to need is already inside our self–we simply need to learn to go within, then choose to go within to rediscover and remember the higher part of the self. We are not really taught in our early years to trust what is within us. We often look outside ourselves for the solutions to the mysteries of life. Yes, we can find the answers to life's questions in the outside world, for those who are known as our spirit guides will speak to us in ways that we have a point of reference–such as how the lyrics of a song or finding a penny on a sidewalk might jar a memory that leads us down a path toward the solution we were seeking. However, the direction we may need to take and the knowingness of that direction would be better served if it were to come from within. We need only to allow it to come to us.

Does the seed spawned from a fruit tree spend the winter days in wonder of what may come to pass in the spring as it nestles beneath the snow? Nature possesses an instinctive quality of knowing what it needs to do in order to create the outcome it desires for any given thing. If this holds true in nature, do we not possess the same ability since we are supposedly the highest on the evolutionary scale in terms of Earthly beings? We do possess the same knowingness as the intelligence encoded in that seed, the same intelligence that causes it to grow into a tree; it simply knows it will become a tree.

ADIO

Above, **D**own, **I**nside, **O**ut. This philosophy stems from the Chiropractic school of healthcare. If we look to the word, not as an acronym but as A Dio, it would be translated as "with God," the All That Is. *May we look Above and bring Down, for the answers are Inside that we may project Out.* And this repeats in the circle of life. If the glyph for infinity, which looks like the number 8 on its side, is turned upward, it signifies the flow of energy coming from above and moving down into the human, then returning to the Heavens only to rejuvenate and return to us. I find that in nature, there are these subtle representations of messages from the Heavens and reminders of the Spiritual Love that is all encompassing.

For example, if we were to look at the Sun's position at its highest point on any day and note that position and do the same every consecutive day over the course of a calendar year, we would notice that connecting the plotted points would form a figure eight (the sign that represents infinity). As an astrologer, I interpret this subtle innuendo to mean that the answers are in the

Heavens, and this is one of the reminders from the Universe that we are not alone.

The dimension of Knowing allows us to look inside ourselves for validation. The reinforcement may come from an outside source, but the source of that validation must come from within the self. It becomes second nature to follow the gut instinct. We may also gain psychic receptivity and psychic faculties from those cosmic experiences, as psychic aspects are part of this twelfth dimension of the human potential.

These experiences come from what we would call Intuition: this is Knowing despite the lack of physical evidence, sometimes even contrary to physical evidence. Intuition is the gut instinct; it could be why, as we are driving, we decide, without apparent reason, to turn left at an intersection where we might not normally make a turn, only later to discover we avoided a significant traffic delay or, even more profoundly, a serious accident. When we are in tune with the Universal vibrations, we can sense, feel, know these instincts to be true. Using this same car example, had we experienced a period of mental anguish prior to that moment at the intersection–stress, anxiety, anger because of those worldly things we deal with–we may not hear what our instincts are telling us. We do not become Aware.

It is my observation that when we experience a crisis over a period of time, we find ourselves entangled in the "thick of things." We come to a point where the daily chaos and stress removes us from a state of peace and harmony, thus leading us to the crisis. This is an extremely simple explanation of something that may, at times, be vastly complicated.

Universal consciousness is, on the Universal scale, humanity understanding the effects of their individual existence and how that existence is affecting the whole of humanity. This is, again, the Knowing that we're not separate from the greater whole. Everything we do is a part of that whole and affects it. Just as a glass of water adds to the volume of the ocean even if we don't notice the displacement–yet we know it has occurred–so, too, are the effects of our thoughts and existence in the whole of humanity. Why don't we realize that?

ETHEREAL VS. PHYSICAL

Before we progressed into the state of being that we now define as Knowing, we were dealing with reality on a physical level. Although we are humans existing in physical form, there remains the invariable connection to the etheric dimension. We experience that dimension during times of prayer, meditation, and the dream state. And some try to reach the etheric dimension through the use of substances, a manner not necessarily serving the highest good for all concerned. These low-level, substance-inspired experiences open doors to dark energy, most of which seem to go undetected and may cause some of the unexplainable disturbances in our lives.

Disrupted sleep, unclear thinking, and poor digestion are all examples that can be attributed partially to low-level negative entities surrounding and attaching themselves to a person.

Even though we are physical in our being, those who have crossed to the etheric plane continually surround us. Psychics and mediums validate that our loved ones who have gone before us remain connected to the essence of our being. And just like in the physical world, there are also those beings on the etheric plane who may not have our best interest in mind. As we move closer to this New Age I spoke of in chapter eleven, we will be more cognizant of these beings and how we can remain centered and grounded so as not to be affected in a negative manner.

BALANCE WITH KNOWING

As we move along the evolutionary scale of human potential, we become conscious of the Knowing that we are a part of the intangible universe. It is intangible because as we envelop this human condition, the wholeness of this Universe is outside the scope of what we can envision. I see this as a positive direction humanity can choose to follow in the years to come, if only proceeded with Awareness so that the positive change that may come to pass among humanity can be reflected onto the collective consciousness of our society.

As humanity advances into the coming years, we will

observe noticeable changes in the levels of energy as it applies to humanity. Those who have a high psychic sensitivity are already experiencing these power surges of energy. It will be necessary for those healers and light workers to be of a high-energy vibration in order for them to have the gift to offset any negative energy that will come to pass.

These healers and light workers can be just about anyone. Typically, they may call themselves psychics, astrologers, and reiki masters, just to name a few. But there are also those whose healing qualities could be classified as something outside of New Age abilities. Someone in the nursing profession can be a light worker, encouraging their patients to look beyond the traditional medicine that may not be healing their illness. These individuals can be anyone who feel this connection to the center of the Universe and who possess the Knowingness, regardless of how they choose to demonstrate it. Through their very personal expression, they will influence the betterment of humanity.

Again, this negative energy is the polar opposite of the positive charge, just like in a battery. Both polarities must be present in order for the battery to operate properly and both polarities must be in balance with each other, as all things must be in humanity. These light workers will create balance through their individual positive energy, offsetting that which can be negative–in whatever form that negativity may be demonstrated.

However, we must not assume this burden should weigh solely on those who have come to this Earth as light workers; instead, the responsibility lies with all of humanity.

THE LIGHT WITHIN...AND WITHOUT

The multi-leveled energy field that radiates from the physical of the human body is known as the human aura, which reflects the moods, personality, characteristics, emotions, general well-being, spiritual abilities, and evolution of any individual. It is made up of several layers reflecting and relating to the chakras (specific energy points of the body), as well as the aspects of our Spiritual and physical life and the environment in which we live.

If we consider the Earth to be the larger organism of which we are a part, the human aura can be equated to the electromagnetic field of our Earth, radiating particles of the self out into the consciousness and cosmicness of humanity, out to the Universe and back to the self of the Earth. This unseen energy field encircling our planet is much the same as the human aura surrounding the physical body.

Sometimes, when particles travel from the sun and bombard the earth's energy field, it creates a light show, similar to the human aura, called the Aurora Borealis and Aurora Australis. However, unlike the way the human aura is created outward from the physical body, these magnificent displays of light are not created outward from the Earth, but rather from the Sun. The real similarity between the human aura and the Earth's auroras is in how the energy field surrounding the Earth simulates the Aura surrounding the body.

There is great parallel in the words *aura* and *Aurora*, which adds to the metaphysical connection of the fundamental nature of these two etheric manifestations. On the Periodic Table of Elements, the symbol Au represents gold. When one is of an extremely high vibration, the aura will radiate a golden glow, as will, at times, the Aurora Borealis. These brilliant displays of radiant light shining in the nighttime sky are another one of nature's messages from the Heavens demonstrating our connection to the All That Is.

Many of those who operate at a high psychic vibration have the ability to see this energy field of the human aura. If you have ever looked at the flame of a candle and noticed a glow around the flame, this is exactly how a human aura represents itself. At times, it may radiate different colors dependant upon the conditions in one's life. Auras are similar to the mood rings of the 1960s that changed hue with body-temperature fluctuations, but are instead tied to the spirit's energy fluctuations, as this is the true representation of the etheric spirit enveloped in the human form. All the happenings in one's life, as well as the individual's loved ones who have crossed to the next dimension, will be apparent in one's aura field.

With the development of Kirlian photography, this

radiant display of light that emanates from the body can be captured on a special type of film. Kirlian photography records the energy flow of any living organism and can assist in diagnosis of inexplicable illnesses; any problem areas in one's body will be obvious in the human aura. Many psychics will read a person's aura to provide the individual with some understanding about what may be happening in his life.

This magnificent display of energy can radiate up to fifty feet or more from one's physical body. We sense this as heat when we are close to someone, but this sensation is more profound than just temperature radiating from the body like the warmth from a radiator. This is the life force, source, the interconnectivity humanity possesses within itself and with all things living; we are all interwoven in the fabric of each other's aura field.

YA GOTTA HAVE FAITH

Most reference material will define faith as allegiance or loyalty to a cause or person or complete confidence and trust in a person or plan. These definitions place the power of faith outside of the self. I would choose to redefine this concept of faith from my metaphysical perspective. I believe the power of faith comes from within the individual self. Not from some external force, but from the force that is within the self.

As I have abundantly stated: we, as humans, are all one; we are not separate from the greatness, the Allness, the All That Is, the magnificent power that created the Heavens and the Earth. We, too, possess that same power within our selves. The Knowing of this concept will cause one to understand that faith in the self, which is where the truth of faith resides. Faith is not external, not from some great power from above, but rather is in co-existence and co-creation with that power from above and within.

Simply stated, faith is Knowing and Knowing is faith. This comes from within the self, not external of the self. When we are taught to place our faith in God, we would be better served to place that faith in the self, rather than outside the self; we would walk with greater confidence, fully aware that we walk within the power of the creation of our realities.

Faith is the ultimate end that has no beginning. As this chapter represents a seeming end to this material, it can, in fact, be the beginning of the greatness of our existence. And the Knowing of this truth will create the beginning of another chapter of our realities.

SPIRITUAL LOVE

Evolving to higher levels of human experience allows our knowingness to manifest a sense of euphoria and the condition of Spiritual Love. This transcends romance, affairs of the heart, and Love with all its Earthly trappings and conditions. This is a Universal Love, a Spiritual Love. It is Love in its purest form, all encompassing, never in prejudice or judgments.

Love in its purest form is the condition so many of us, while wearing this human flesh, strive to attain and achieve with one another, and even more so with our lover/beloved partner. Though this is not something unattainable, many do feel this experience is beyond their realm of possibility. I would say "Nonsense!" Nevertheless, it is a condition that must be chosen. However, true spiritual love as it exists among the All That Is simply just *is*–just like the All That Is. This condition of emotion transcends this Earthly dimension and becomes not an emotion of Earthly form, but a condition of the spiritual realm.

I was once asked, "Who do you think we first meet when we cross over to the other side?" My reply was that we meet and are greeted by everyone we have ever loved and who has loved us. I would also include those who, while in Earthly form, we have labeled as enemies and opponents. In that dimension of the Spirit Kingdom, in absolute reality, the only thing that exists is love in its purest form.

HEAVEN: A PLACE ON EARTH?

Have you ever traveled to a place where you feel such an indescribable peace and tranquility that it almost seems to be not of this Earth? This location may be far from where we live, or it can be as close as our backyards. For me, it is when I am by the sea. I find the sea to be the place where I can go to become peaceful, to rejuvenate and revitalize my spirit, and to be in communion with nature. I look to the sea in need and it returns its magnitude and strength to me, its power and force. The transfer of energy is much like the yin and the yang of life, like the tides that rise and recede, like the ebb and flow of river water flowing into the ocean, and like the waxing and waning of the Moon's cycles.

For me, this is what I have come to know as Heaven, or as close as I can get while I encompass this body. It isn't the actual physical place that reminds me of Heaven, but rather the sensation that comes to me from being at the sea. The solitude and euphoria that my spirit experiences are what I would know to be Heaven.

The experience of Heaven is as unique as each individual in this human condition. When we do experience Heaven, this state of being will also be as individual as our humanness, at least until we are all combined in the unification of the Allness and we recall the oneness of that which we are. Then, we do it all again. The never-ending, all-encompassing cycles of the energies of all the planets, stars, galaxies, quasars and quarks. This is the All That Is, and Heaven is the Allness.

KNOWING AND NOW

When we come from a state of Knowing, we learn to live in the now. We remove our thoughts from our actions of the past and we stop looking for better days ahead. In a 1997 song, Dave Mathews sang: "The future is no place to place your better days." So simple, yet so profoundly true.

When we find ourselves experiencing–reliving–the past or living in a fantasized future in our minds, imagining what can bring us true happiness, we are actually forgetting that which is already present in our sphere of beauty. We allow the present to pass us by. In other words, take time to smell the roses; that rose may not be there for you to experience its beauty tomorrow.

Through so many of our days, we find ourselves hurried, rushed about, only to awaken one day to realize that our children have grown and our hair is silver-gray. Many times we say to the self, "I will be happy when I have more money," or "I will be fulfilled when I find my beloved." When we exist in the condition of Knowing, we simply just understand that all we desire will manifest itself in our lives, all the hopes and wishes will be created, for when we have reached the state of Knowing, we will have made the choices to achieve our desires. When we come to a place of Knowing, all our worldly requirements have been fulfilled and the appreciation for the beauty of each day will become more profound.

ALL THAT IS *IS* ALL THERE IS

We have now reached a higher level of consciousness, the plane of existence upon which few may choose to travel. The higher self of the spiritual being exists in a state of Knowing, a state engulfed by peace, harmony, and spiritual love. This is the true essence of the human in a state of being who is operating at his highest vibration. Neptune and the sign Pisces are representations of this state of being. This dimension of the human potential is the most abstract, intangible, and elusive–as Neptune can be–because we are dealing with spirit and not the physical human form. When we choose to lift the fog of illusion of the ego, then we can come to know the essence of the true self.

In the beginning of this book, my journal about human potential, we touched upon the archetypes and the Akashic Records where all the outcomes of all the possibilities exist. And in this Knowing, our Universal connections, is where we discover how, in this aspect of the human potential, we have the ability to rediscover the Allness.

Herein this book lies all that is. Here, within each of us, lies the potential of the All That Is, if we so choose to realize that potential.

Blessed Be.

Conclusion

*Everything science has taught me—and
continues to teach me—strengthens my
belief in the continuity of our spiritual
existence after death. Nothing disappears
without a trace.*
—WERNHER VON BRAUN

I am an astrologer, metaphysician, spiritual and holistic practitioner, and a member of this race we call human. I see all things through my astrologer's eyes and in that understanding, in part with our unique composition created by the planetary imprint at the moment of our birth, I have come to learn these twelve dimensions of potential in the human experience.

As it is observed from the Earth, the Heavens have been divided into twelve sectors, hence the twelve signs of the zodiac. A circle is complete at 360 degrees, so if there are twelve slices in the astrological pie, each will measures thirty degrees. These twelve dimensions covered in this book characterize each area of the Earthly life. Every aspect of life is located somewhere within these twelve dimensions. All the pieces of that pie are located somewhere in the sphere of the human experience, i.e., the human potential. There is potential, opportunity, and greatness in all experiences, if that is what we choose to observe.

As I have stated in the beginning and now again in the end, the number twelve is of a high spiritual vibration. As we come to know and understand these twelve aspects of the human potential within the fabric of our being, we begin to function at a higher Spiritual vibration. The process of the creation of this book unfolded in three trimesters of twelve weeks. As it relates to Indian Numerology, the number three refers to "an artist who will infuse, inspire, and pull society upward and forward through idealistic contributions."* I found this definition very apropos as it relates to this path I have chosen for my life's mission, particularly because my early life experiences originate from an art background.

I was in a place of a high spirit vibration when my muse bestowed upon me the inspiration for this book. This revelation came to me in part because of my desire to create something that would influence humanity through the realization of the human potential, which resides in each and every human being.

How and where did all this begin and how was human-

---

*This Indian Numerology characteristic was provided by Christina Richa Devi, a teacher of Vedic Numerology, for the web pages of the www.sanatansociety.org site.

ity, in its earliest of stages, inspired to come to this understanding? Well, that would be the topic for another great journal. Records of astrological understandings date back to the times of Mesopotamia. Before the Old Testament and before the Torah, there existed a time when the practice and understanding of metaphysics and astrology was as common then as it is uncommon now. Of course, it was quite different then.

Today's astrology, as we have come to know and understand it, has evolved over the millennia in how it relates to the human condition and the understanding of such concepts. I believe these astrological principles have been divinely inspired over the course of history and will continue to be modified as the years continue to pass. Even the simplest household appliance comes with an instruction manual; why would the All That Is have created this human experience without the proper tools for its operation?

Each of the twelve dimensions of this human potential has an opposite so that it, as does nature, creates a dynamic balance, a yin and yang, an ebb and flow of all things in symmetry and perfection. In the way that one must experience something hot to understand cold, a similar principle applies to all experiences of the human condition. To experience a loss from death lends a greater appreciation to birth, and to life. And if we are to know love that is in its purest sense, in its highest form of divinity, there are moments when, perhaps, we must experience something ghastly and deceitful. That is not to say that we cannot experience a true form of love without this incident; however, the understanding of its opposite lends a greater sense of Knowing to the experience. As I illustrated over and again, each aspect of the human potential has a counterbalance for its dynamic.

If we could exist in a place where our being understands trusting our instincts, we would easily call upon the ability to create balance in any aspect of our lives where it is lacking. A beneficial and positive outcome from living in this manner would be an existence of peace and harmony. When musical numbers contain multiple lines of melody that seem to just "fit" with each other, harmony has been created. Life can be equally harmonious. Just like a choir, when all beings seem to fluently sing together, each listening to the others so that every spirit knows when the time arrives for them to sing their parts, humanity experiences itself in all its greatest potential.

When we evolve to the point where we realize and understand the potential that lies within each human being, we then begin to live an existence of greater depth and profoundness. We do not see life as a win/lose situation, but rather as a win/win experience. We do not fear that one will take something from another or that unless I hurt you first, you will hurt me. If we live in a civilization that is highly evolved, we will not be concerned with borders, for in demonstrating that concern, we simply exhibit our selves as thinking we are separate from one another and that we have something to lose. But in truth, we each, as individuals, possess the same human potential, and as individuals, we are also all part of the same oneness, the All That Is. There is no real separation between individuals.

Here I have described my understanding of the human potential that has unfolded through my Earthly experience. It is with these words that I hope to inspire everyone who reads them to look within themselves, see the potential that may lie within the individuality of the spirit, and realize their potential so that we all may exist in a place of Knowing, for we are all one.

Namaste.

Recommendations by the Authors

Authors Ray and Carlo would like to share some books and web sites they have come across that have inspired them or that they believe propose interesting perspectives on our world and the changes that are occurring within it.

RECOMMENDED READING

The Celestine Prophecy – James Redfield

Conversations with God (the series) – Neale Donald Walsch

The Courage to be Rich: Creating a Life of Material and Spiritual Abundance – Suze Orman

Don't Sweat the Small Stuff...and it's all small stuff – Richard Carlson, Ph.D.

Further Along the Road Less Traveled: The Unending Journey Toward Spiritual Growth – M. Scott Peck

If the Buddha Dated – Charlotte Kasl

The Last Hours of Ancient Sunlight – Thom Hartman

The Laws of Money, the Lessons of Life: Keep What You Have and Create What You Deserve – Suze Orman

A New Earth: Awakening to Your Life's Purpose – Eckhart Tolle

The Path to Love – Deepak Chopra

People of the Lie: The Hope for Healing Human Evil – M. Scott Peck

The Power of Your Subconscious Mind – Dr. Joseph Murphy

The Prophet – Kahlil Gibran

The Road Less Traveled: A New Psychology of Love, Traditional Values, and Spiritual Growth – M. Scott Peck

The Seven Spiritual Laws of Success: A Practical Guide to the Fulfillment of Your Dreams – Deepak Chopra

What the Bleep Do We Know!?: Discovering the Endless Possibilities for Altering Your Everyday Reality – William Arntz, Betsy Chasse, Mark Vicente

Who Moved My Cheese? – Spencer Johnson, M.D.

Who Would I Be If I Weren't So Afraid – Dr. Ginger Grancagnolo

You Can't Afford the Luxury of a Negative Thought – John Roger & Peter McWilliams

RECOMMENDED WEB SITES

Center to Self Reliance – www.centertoselfreliance.com

The Millennium Campaign – www.millenniumcampaign.org

One – www.one.org

The Sanatan Society – www.sanatansociety.org

Printed in the United States
59842LVS00003B/13-84